Prayer

Berkeley Hills Books
Titles by M. K. Gandhi

The Bhagavad Gita According to Gandhi
Book of Prayers
Prayer
Vows and Observances
The Way to God

Prayer

MOHANDAS K. GANDHI

Edited by John Strohmeier
Foreword by Arun Gandhi
Introduction by Michael N. Nagler

Berkeley Hills Books
Berkeley, California

Published by
Berkeley Hills Books
P. O. Box 9877
Berkeley, California 94709
www.berkeleyhills.com

Comments on this book may be addressed to:
rob@berkeleyhills.com

Cover design by Elysium, San Francisco.
Cover Photo © CORBIS/Bettman.
Manufactured in the United States of America.
Distributed by Publishers Group West.

Library of Congress Cataloging-in-Publication Data

Gandhi, Mahatma, 1869-1948.
    Prayer / Mohandas K. Gandhi ; edited by John Strohmeier ; foreword
by Arun Gandhi ; introduction by Michael N. Nagler.
    p. cm.
    ISBN 1-893163-09-1 (alk. paper)
    1. Prayer--Hinduism. 2. Hinduism--Rituals. I. Strohmeier, John. II.
Title.

BL1236.36 .G36 2000
294.5'43--dc21   00-034223

Contents

Part II. Forms and Methods of Prayer

Part III. Ramanama: The Repetition of God's Name

Prayer was first compiled and edited by Chandrakant Kaji and published in India in 1977 by the Navajivan Publishing House. This first North American edition has been edited to conform to American spelling and usage, and slightly abridged from the original so that it more directly addresses concerns of western readers.

Foreword

ARUN GANDHI

Writing a foreword to this collection of M. K. Gandhi's writings on prayer is a daunting task. I am not sure I am qualified to analyze his thoughts on religious matters. It is, therefore, with humility that I offer some opinions and observations.

Grandfather's belief in God and prayers was legendary, and to some extent, misunderstood. Many people, including eminent analysts, could not fathom his love of secularism on the one hand and, on the other, his frequent references to Ramrajya — the kingdom of Rama — as an ideal for India. Even Jawaharlal Nehru, the first Prime Minister of India and an heir to Gandhian thought, questioned the creation of Ramrajya in an India where Muslims, Christians and Buddhists made up a substantial segment of the population.

To understand this, one must recognize that Ramrajya to Grandfather did not signify a Hindu state at all. He saw in Lord Rama a votary of truth and justice. During Rama's legendary reign there was equality for all, there were no rich and no poor, no one with power and no one helpless. There is nothing Hindu about this concept. It is part of every religious faith in the world and an aspiration that everyone shares. Grandfather used the term Ramrajya because it was one that a vast majority of the Indian population, including Muslims and Christians, understood and appreciated.

The successful campaigns that Grandfather launched for freedom and equal rights clearly establish him as an astute politician with an uncanny ability to gauge the temper of the people and inspire them to action. He knew precisely the time, the place and the method that would be most effective. No politician could overlook the fact that more than eighty per cent of Indians belong to the Hindu faith, that almost an equal number live in poverty, and that their only source of knowledge is what they learn from wandering minstrels. Consequently, when someone touches their hearts these simple folk follow.

Grandfather accepted this reality. To earn the confidence of the people he had to speak their language and be like them. This is not to suggest that he lacked conviction. Even when he did something with a political purpose he did so with full understanding and acceptance. He could not have moved the masses of India as he did without truth and sincerity as his guiding principles. He appealed to all Indians to believe in religious heroes, advising Christians, Muslims, Buddhists, Jains, Hindus and Sikhs to follow their scriptures with the same understanding and conviction.

Through his all-inclusive prayers Grandfather brought these people together and bound them in love and understanding. Prayers were, to him, a dialogue with God which had to be kept with utmost solemnity at the appointed time every day. Wherever he was, every morning and evening, he insisted on his communion with God. Nothing was ever so important as to distract him from this. People have commented on this derisively but it is an indication of his faith and sincerity.

Grandfather believed the only way to world peace — and peace of the individual — was through love, respect, understanding and acceptance of each other and our religious beliefs. I hope the reader finds Grandfather's writings on God and prayer inspirational and informative. The only way one can truly accept and appreciate their innate wisdom is by approaching his writings with an open and receptive mind.

Introduction

MICHAEL N. NAGLER

We tend to think of prayer today as either the most important thing a person can do or just about the most irrelevant. Both are right, Gandhi would say. Prayer is the most irrelevant thing we can do when it's the mechanical repetition of mere words, but when it's the expression of a heartfelt desire to be closer to God, nothing we do could be more relevant.

When the words become felt symbols of a deeply held reality, the act of prayer can deepen the worshipper's concentration until, shutting out everything but what a fourteenth-century English mystic called the "naked intent of love," he or she can lose all separate identity in the eternally Real, or in religious language, come face to face with the awesome being of God revealed in the depths of his or her consciousness. This state no one would call irrelevant. As Gandhi shows here (and in the wider record of his life) it changes everything.

That the word "prayer" can mean such widely different things is not a new phenomenon, not only a feature of our materialistic culture. A great expert on prayer from the seventh century of our era, St. Isaac of Syria, wrote, "Some of the fathers called this 'doing silence of the heart'; others called it 'attention'; yet others 'sobriety' and 'opposition' [to thoughts]; while others called it 'examining thoughts' and 'guarding the mind.' . . . The Fathers called the same thing by many names."

Today we try to sort things out by using the word "prayer" for an act of words, usually a petition of some kind, and calling the extreme state of absorption I just referred to — a state that goes beyond words entirely — "meditation." One only has to look at the famous photograph of Gandhi at prayer reproduced on the cover of this book to know that in fact he was meditating. The utter peace and inward absorption are unmistakable.

At the risk of further complicating things, Gandhi will refer here to yet another technique that has been used down the ages to concentrate the mind on the supreme reality and was particularly well developed in the devotional tradition of India: the time-honored technique of silently repeating a concise formula, or even a single word, expressing a name or attribute of God — Ramanama.

As anyone who has read *The Way of a Pilgrim* can testify, this technique was far from unknown in the Christian West. East or West, the relationship between repetition of a mantram and meditation seems to depend on the system of meditation one is learning. As I learned them, meditation and the mantram are complementary, to be used at different times. For the fourteenth-century authority I just cited, the anonymous author of *The Cloud of Unknowing*, if you have trouble focusing your mind on your "naked intent" toward the Being of God, go ahead and use a single word like "God" or "love" — just what Gandhi recommends in a passage we will be discussing shortly. Elsewhere, however, he is less precise. The reason for this, to quote Irénée Hausherr, "those few ascetics who have left some record of their prayer life . . . all knew that what counts most is the interior disposition, not the material formula."

One thing, however, is perfectly clear. The repetition of the mantram, which in Gandhi's case was the the name of the god Rama, is a key to what he became. It is his "infallible remedy." Nothing that he achieved can be understood without understanding the rootedness of his being in the supreme truth, for which this simple technique of repeating its name all but incessantly was the foundation. The fact that he doggedly repeated that name until it became as intimate to him as his very breath made it possible for him to retain his awareness of truth, his God, in the midst of the most trying and turbulent times. When that otherwise unknown woman, his nurse Rambha, taught the fearful child Mohan to use the mantram to dispel his fear of ghosts, how could she have suspected that this gift would be a seed of the greatest revolution of modern times?

This brings up an interesting dilemma. When one looks to Gandhi as an authority on prayer, which he certainly was, it can bring up the apparent contradiction that prayer is supposed to be the ultimate quietism. But Gandhi is the ultimate activist — the great *karmayogi*. When does a man who worked fifteen hours a day, seven days a week, for fifty years, get time to pray? How does a man who tore down a world order and in its place founded over 1,200 institutions that are still going concerns in India today, who got by on 3-4 hours sleep and kept up a frightening pace well into his seventies, relax? The answer is that prayer is not relaxation. It is the "work," as our fourteenth-century authority calls it, of bringing the titanic factory of the mind to a standstill. But more than that, even work, paradoxically enough, is relaxing — at least when you do it the way Gandhi did, by throwing himself into everything he did with passion, and yet so little thought of himself that his "I" was completely absorbed into the meaning of the task. There is an interesting comment by a spiritual teacher whose community Gandhiji visited during a tour of South India:

> When you look at him you can see that he is absorbed in yoga, for whenever he looks at something he pays all his attention. He never glances at anything else. Many other leaders came with him, but they were looking everywhere, as if they had five or six pairs of eyes.

For Gandhi, action draws directly on the power of interior quiet, while acting entirely for others erodes the greatest obstruction to that quiet — the ego. In the Christian tradition there is a story about a novice monk who asked his preceptor, "If everything depends on God, why should we work; and if everything depends on us, why should we pray?" The teacher replied, "Work as if everything depended on you, and pray as if everything depended on God." We can almost hear Gandhi chuckling.

So we see that prayer, in this important book, means everything from a more or less mechanical repetition or idle wish to the supreme state of absorption striven for by the mystics — and many techniques and stages in between. Because one can get to that absorbed state of meditation through prayer, the word stands for the whole process, but it is important to remember that for Gandhi himself real prayer meant that latter state. "The essence of all prayers [is] to establish God in [our] heart." And this is not something to do just on one occasion or in one particular setting. "When a man has got to the stage of heart prayer, he prays always, whether in . . . secret or in the multitude."

This comment about being in a state of heart prayer even "in the multitude" was the subject of some dispute. If one is reaching for a state of utter quiet, the objection often arose, what is the use of crowding in with a group of other people and praying aloud? Here we begin to appreciate the tolerance of Gandhiji's approach to the spiritual life, which balances his uncompromising insistence that unless your mind is still and your heart is absorbed in the goal you are not praying. That is true, but before you reach that goal, the traditional aids handed down in all religions are not only not wrong, they're necessary. He who overthrew so many institutions because of their structural violence was no iconoclast when it came to the traditional methods of religious practice. He was well aware that the vast majority of us need some sort of external aid to begin intensifying our concentration. Thus when challenged by purists who tended to scorn aids like praying aloud he pointed out beautifully that, "Prayer is a function of the heart. We speak aloud in order to wake it up." "When we speak out loud at prayer time, our speech is addressed not to God but to ourselves, and is intended to shake off our torpor."

Congregational prayer can bond together people into a real community — a major plus for Gandhi, whose prayer meetings embraced people from all religions. "For a congregational life a congregational prayer is a necessity." It could even help certain people to get to the final goal, which was always "to establish God in [our] heart." But for this purpose serious members of the ashram would also do individual prayer, just as a singer has to practice his or her part before joining the choir.

When in his "weakness" Gandhi prayed for the life of his son Manilal, he addressed a prayer to an external God even though he knew that in reality God is within us. Was that wrong? "We are aware of the presence of God in our heart, and in order to shake off attachment we for the moment think of God as different from ourselves and pray to him." This is Gandhi at his best, knowing human weakness, working with it, and above all, first of all, in himself. This is more than tolerance; it's compassion.

Western adepts have known that petitionary prayer, while not the goal, could be a step. When a Christian teacher was asked why we should pray when God already knows what we want, he replied, "The point of prayer is not to tell God what we want, but to get ourselves ready to receive it." Gandhi subscribes to this view. When he prayed for Manilal's recovery, "it was a sign not of wisdom but of a father's love. There is really only one prayer that we may offer: 'Thy will be done'."

And yet even this state of petition, where the worshipper lays him or herself open in complete detachment to the will of God, is not the final stage. In the words of St. Antony the Great, "That prayer is not perfect in which the monk is conscious of himself or of the fact that he is praying." Or as Gandhiji puts it, "In heartfelt prayer the worshipper's attention is concentrated on the object of worship so much so that he is not conscious of anything else." So when prayer becomes meditation (to use our terms), the time must come when the words of the prayer or hymn or inspirational passage are suspended, taking with them all the background noise of the mind. Most Christian writers after the Middle Ages called it the "prayer of silence." A Desert Father describes the indescribable result:

> "And when my tongue becomes silent because of the sweetness that comes from understanding them [the words of the psalm or gospel] . . . I fall into a state where my senses and my thoughts become inactive. When by prolonged stillness my heart becomes tranquil and undisturbed by the turmoil of recollections, waves of joy ceaselessly surge over me, waves arising from inward intuitions that beyond expectation suddenly blossom forth to delight my heart."

Gandhi's touch is to treat all this with down-to-earth practicality. Even when he makes his most inspiring claims, as he once wrote about having heard the voice of God, he was stating "a simple, scientific truth" which, "can be tested by all who have the will and the patience to acquire the necessary qualifications."

This volume, first published in 1977 in India, brings together Gandhi's observations, reflections and exhortations on prayer in all its meanings, and comes close to being the book on spiritual life that he never had the chance to write. It is the testimony of a man who not only lived that life to its highest conclusion but forged of his most intimate experiences an instrument of social reconstruction for millions of others. Meditators will easily relate to the cheek-by-jowl juxtaposition, so like Gandhi, of the highest inspiration and the nitty-grittiest tips on how to climb the steep heights of prayer in the modern world.

In the little essay on group prayer he began to sketch out in 1932, for example, reproduced here on pages 144-145, he begins emphatically, with the essential point, "Prayer is the very foundation of the ashram." Then the discourse flows, in his typical sliding transitions, from point to practical point.

* To be real, prayer has to be "from the heart,"
* so no one should doze during prayers (Do we drift off while we're eating?).
* No one should miss a prayer meeting (Do we forget a meal? In prayer, regularity is even more essential.).
* If your attention drifts while at prayers, you are as good as absent,
* so don't just rush to the meeting — get up fully, brush your teeth, and resolve your mind to stay alert.
* Here's how to sit, breathe, and do the recitation without drifting.
* You can repeat Ramanama (i.e., the mantram) if all else fails,
* and if even that fails, stand up. (But this is embarrassing — so, with trademark Gandhian compassion)
* Every now and then some of the adults should stand up even when they're not drowsy, to remove the stigma. And finally, as we began,
* no mechanical repetition. "Even if a person does not know Sanskrit, he should learn the meaning of each verse and meditate over it."

Here he is, ticking off a list of tips as humdrum as brushing your teeth and sitting straight, but in the authenticity of those very details you sense the determination, the passion, the one-pointed focus he brought to everything surrounding prayer, when most of us seem to "have five or six pairs of eyes." Perhaps it is because whatever he has to say is grounded in his own repeated, lived experience and his desire to share it with us is driven by his "insatiable love for mankind." Whatever the reason, the effect of the thoughts here collected make life-altering reading. Let his inspiration and his practicality strengthen your own practice, and decide for yourself whether prayer is the most irrelevant thing a person can do today or the most important.

Prayer

O God, thy law is mysterious.
Wherever the heart is set, there thou art to be seen;
with thee there is neither temple nor mosque.
Thou lookest only for a true heart in thy seeker.
Thou exhibitest the splendour of thy love
to him who has surrendered himself heart and soul to thee.
He who becomes enamoured of thy divine qualities
takes all his colouring from thee.
He in whom there is still egotism left
is like one who has lost his way,
and he is united to thee who has lost his egotism.
He who believes in thee sees thee face to face.
It is like a beggar finding a priceless pearl.

Part I.
The Meaning of and
Necessity for Prayer

I. The Core of Life

I am glad that you all want me to speak to you on the meaning of and the necessity for prayer. I believe that prayer is the very soul and essence of religion, and, therefore, prayer must be the very core of the life of man, for no man can live without religion. There are some who in the egotism of their reason declare that they have nothing to do with religion. But it is like a man saying that he breathes but that he has no nose. Whether by reason, or by instinct, or by superstition, man acknowledges some sort of relationship with the divine. The rankest agnostic or atheist does acknowledge the need of a moral principle, and associates something good with its observance and something bad with its nonobservance. Bradlaugh, whose atheism is well known, always insisted on proclaiming his innermost conviction. He had to suffer a lot for thus speaking the truth, but he delighted in it and said that truth is its own reward. Not that he was quite insensible to the joy resulting from the observance of truth. This joy, however, is not at all worldly, but springs out of communion with the divine. That is why I have said that even a man who disowns religion cannot and does not live without religion.

Now I come to the next thing, viz., that prayer is the very core of man's life, as it is the most vital part of religion. Prayer is either petitional or in its wider sense is inward communion. In either case the ultimate result is the same. Even when it is petitional, the petition should be for the cleansing and purification of the soul, for freeing it from the layers of ignorance and darkness that envelop it. He, therefore, who hungers for the awakening of the divine in him must fall back on prayer. But prayer is no mere exercise of words or of the ears, it is no mere repetition of empty formula. Any amount of repetition of Ramanama [God's Name] is futile if it fails to stir the soul. It is better in prayer to have a heart without words than words without a heart. It must be in clear response to the spirit which hungers for it. And even as a hungry man relishes a hearty meal, a hungry soul will relish a heartfelt prayer. And I am giving you a bit of my experience and that of my companions when I say that he who has experienced the magic of prayer may do without food for days together but not a single moment without prayer. For without prayer there is no inward peace.

If that is the case, someone will say, we should be offering our prayers every minute of our lives. There is no doubt about it, but we, erring mortals, who find it difficult to retire within ourselves for inward communion even for a single moment, will find it impossible to remain perpetually in communion with the divine. We, therefore, fix some hours when we make a serious effort to throw off the attachments of the world for a while, we make a serious endeavor to remain, so to say, out of the flesh. You have heard Surdas' hymn [page 179]. It is the passionate cry of a soul hungering for union with the divine. According to our standards he was a saint, but according to his own he was a proclaimed sinner. Spiritually he was miles ahead of us, but he felt the separation from the divine so keenly that he has uttered that anguished cry in loathing and despair.

I have talked of the necessity for prayer, and therethrough I have dealt with the essence of prayer. We are born to serve our fellow man, and we cannot properly do so unless we are wide awake. There is an eternal struggle raging in man's breast between the powers of darkness and of light, and he who has not the sheet-anchor of prayer to rely upon will be a victim to the powers of darkness. The man of prayer will be at peace with himself and with the whole world. The man who goes about the affairs of the world without a prayerful heart will be miserable and will make the world also miserable. Apart therefore from its bearing on man's condition after death, prayer has incalculable value for man in this world of the living. Prayer is the only means of bringing about orderliness and peace and repose in our daily acts. We inmates of the ashram who came here in search of truth and for insistence on truth professed to believe in the efficacy of prayers, but had never up to now made it a matter of vital concern. We did not bestow on it the care that we did on other matters. I woke from my slumbers one day and realized that I had been woefully negligent of my duty in the matter. I have, therefore, suggested measures of stern discipline and far from being any the worse, I hope we are the better for it. For it is so obvious. Take care of the vital thing and other things will take care of themselves. Rectify one angle of a square, and the other angles will be automatically right.

Begin, therefore, your day with prayer, and make it so soulful that it may remain with you until the evening. Close the day with prayer so that you may have a peaceful night free from dreams and nightmares. Do not worry about the form of prayer. Let it be any form, it should be such as can put us into communion with the divine. Only, whatever be the form, let not the spirit wander while the words of prayer run on out of your mouth.

If what I have said has gone home to you, you will not be at peace until you have compelled your hostel superintendents to interest themselves in your prayer and to make it obligatory. Restraint self-imposed is no compulsion. A man, who chooses the path of freedom from restraint, i.e. of self-indulgence, will be a bond slave of passions, whilst the man who binds himself to rules and restraints releases himself. All things in the universe, including the sun and the moon and the stars, obey certain laws. Without the restraining influence of these laws the world would not go on for a single moment. You, whose mission in life is service of your fellow man, will go to pieces if you do not impose on yourselves some sort of discipline, and prayer is a necessary spiritual discipline. It is discipline and restraint that separates us from the brute. If we will be men walking with our heads erect and not walking on all fours, let us understand and put ourselves under voluntary discipline and restraint.

Young India, January 23, 1930

2. Prayer is Necessary For All

Man's need for prayer is as great as his need for bread. A bad man will use his ears to hear evil of others and see sinful things, but the good man says that had he a thousand eyes and ears, he would use them to contemplate the vision of God forever, and to hear devotional songs, and employ his five thousand tongues to sing his praises. It is only after I have prayed here every day that I feel the bliss of having tasted the food of knowledge. For that man who wishes to be a real human being, dal and roti are not his food. They count little to him. His real food is prayer.

Collected Works — XI (1969), p. 219-20

There can be no manner of doubt that this universe of sentient beings is governed by a law. If you can think of law without its giver, I would say that the law is the lawgiver — that is God. When we pray to the law we simply yearn after knowing the law and obeying it. We become what we yearn after. Hence the necessity for prayer.

The Diary of Mahadev Desai, vol. I (I953), p. 222

The necessity of prayers is a matter of universal experience. If you have faith in them, you will feel interest in them.

Collected Works — XLIV (1971), p. 85

---

3. Man Cannot Live Without Prayer

As food is necessary for the body, prayer is necessary for the soul. A man may be able to do without food for a number of days as Macswinney did for over seventy days—but, believing in God, man cannot, should not, live a moment without prayer. You will say that we see lots of people living without prayer. I dare say they do, but it is the existence of the brute which, for man, is worse than death. I have not the shadow of a doubt that the strife and quarrels with which our atmosphere is so full to-day are due to the absence of the spirit of true prayer. You will demur to the statement, I know, and contend that millions of Hindus, Musalmans and Christians do offer their prayers. It is because I had thought you would raise the objection that I used the words "true prayer."

Hypocrisy of Lip-prayer

The fact is, we have been offering our prayers with the lips but hardly ever with our hearts, and it is to escape, if possible, the hypocrisy of the lip-prayer, that we in the ashram repeat every evening the last verses of the second chapter of the Bhagavad Gita. The condition of the "equable in spirit" that is described in those verses, if we contemplate them daily, is bound slowly to turn our hearts towards God. If you would base your education on the true foundation of a pure character and pure heart, there is nothing so helpful as to offer your prayers every day, truly and religiously.

Young India, December 15, 1927

Prayer is even more essential for the well-being of the soul than is food for the maintenance of the body. It becomes necessary to give up food on occasions in order to benefit the body. But prayer may never be abandoned. If we provide food for the body which is perishable, then, surely, it is our primary duty to provide food for the soul which is imperishable, and such sustenance is found in prayer. The real meaning of prayer is devoted worship.

Food for the Soul (1957), pp. 59-60

[From "Sermon at Kingsley Hall"]

If we believed in God . . . it followed that we must pray to him. Though prayer, it was said, was to the soul what food was to the body, yet prayer was far more important for the soul than food was for the body, because we could at times go without food and the body would feel the better for the fast, but there was no such thing as prayer-fast. . . . We can overindulge in food. But we can never overindulge in prayer.

Collected Works — XLVIII (1972), p. 11

4. The Eternal Duel

A friend writes:

"In the article entitled "The Tangle of Ahimsa," appearing in *Young India* of October 11th, you have stated most forcefully that cowardice and *ahimsa* [nonviolence] are incompatible. There is not an ambiguous syllable in your statement. But may I request that you tell us how cowardice can be exorcised from a man's character? I notice that all characters are but the sum total of habits formed. How are we to undo our old habits and build the new ones of courage, intelligence and action? I am convinced that habits can be destroyed, and better and nobler habits can be formed giving birth to a new character in a person. It seems to me that you know prayers, discipline and studies by which a man can attain a second birth. Won't you kindly tell us about them? Do give us your knowledge and advice in one of the numbers of *Young India.* Please help us by giving an account of the method of praying and working by which a man can recreate himself."

The question refers to the eternal duel that is so graphically described in the Mahabharata under the cloak of history and that is every day going on in millions of breasts. Man's destined purpose is to conquer old habits, to overcome the evil in him and to restore good to its rightful place. If religion does not teach us how to achieve this conquest, it teaches us nothing. But there is no royal road to success in this, the truest enterprise in life. Cowardice is perhaps the greatest vice from which we suffer and is also possibly the greatest violence, certainly far greater than bloodshed and the like that generally go under the name of violence. For it comes from want of faith in God and ignorance of his attributes. But I am sorry that I have not the ability to give "the knowledge and the advice" that the correspondent would have me to give on how to dispel cowardice and other vices. But I can give my own testimony and say that a heartfelt prayer is undoubtedly the most potent instrument that man possesses for overcoming cowardice and all other bad old habits. Prayer is an impossibility without a living faith in the presence of God within.

Christianity and Islam describe the same process as a duel between God and Satan, not outside but within; Zoroastrianism as a duel between Ahurmazd and Ahriman; Hinduism as a duel between forces of good and forces of evil. We have to make our choice whether we should ally ourselves with the forces of evil or with the forces of good. And to pray to God is nothing but that sacred alliance between God and man whereby he attains his deliverance from the clutches of the prince of darkness. But a heartfelt prayer is not a recitation with the lips. It is a yearning from within which expresses itself in every word, every act, nay, every thought of man. When an evil thought successfully assails him, he may know that he offered but a lip-prayer and similarly with regard to an evil word escaping his lips or an evil act done by him. Real prayer is an absolute shield and protection against this trinity of evils. Success does not always attend the very first effort at such real living prayer. We have to strive against ourselves, we have to believe in spite of ourselves, because months are as our years. We have, therefore, to cultivate illimitable patience if we will realize the efficacy of prayer. There will be darkness, disappointment and even worse; but we must have courage enough to battle against all these and not succumb to cowardice. There is no such thing as retreat for a man of prayer.

What I am relating is not a fairy tale. I have not drawn an imaginary picture. I have summed up the testimony of men who have by prayer conquered every difficulty in their upward progress, and I have added my own humble testimony that the more I live the more I realize how much I owe to faith and prayer which is one and the same thing for me. And I am quoting an experience not limited to a few hours, or days or weeks, but extending over an unbroken period of nearly forty years. I have had my share of disappointments, uttermost darkness, counsels of despair, counsels of caution, subtlest assaults of pride; but I am able to say that my faith — and I know that it is still little enough, by no means as great as I want it to be — has ultimately conquered every one of these difficulties up to now. If we have faith in us, if we have a prayerful heart, we may not tempt God, may not make terms with him. We must reduce ourselves to a cipher. Barodadal [the brother of poet Rabindranath Tagore] sent me a precious Sanskrit verse not long before his death. It means impliedly that a man of devotion reduces himself to zero. Not until we have reduced ourselves to nothingness can we conquer the evil in us. God demands nothing less than complete self-surrender as the price for the only real freedom that is worth having. And when a man thus loses himself, he immediately finds himself in the service of all that lives. It becomes his delight and his recreation. He is a new man never weary of spending himself in the service of God's creation.

Young India, December 20, 1928

5. What is Prayer?

A medical graduate asks:

"What is the best form of prayer? How much time should be spent at it? In my opinion to do justice is the best form of prayer and one who is sincere about doing justice to all does not need to do any more praying. Some people spend a long time over *sandhya* [a Sanskrit prayer] and ninety-five percent of them do not understand the meaning of what they say. In my opinion, prayer should be said in one's mother tongue. It alone can affect the soul best. I should say that a sincere prayer for one minute is enough. It should suffice to promise God not to sin."

Prayer means asking God for something in a reverent attitude. But the word is used also to denote any devotional act. Worship is a better term to use for what the correspondent has in mind. But definition apart, what is it that millions of Hindus, Musalmans, Christians and Jews and others do every day during the time set apart for the adoration of the maker? It seems to me that it is a yearning of the heart to be one with the maker, an invocation for his blessing. It is in this case the attitude that matters, not words uttered or muttered.

And often the association of words that have been handed down from ancient times has an effect which in their rendering into one's mother-tongue they will lose altogether. Thus the *Gayatri* [an ancient Hindu hymn to the Sun God] translated and recited in, say, Gujarati, will not have the same effect as the original. The utterance of the word "Rama" will instantaneously affect millions of Hindus, when the word "God," although they may understand the meaning, will leave them untouched. Words after all acquire a power by long usage and sacredness associated with their use. There is much, therefore, to be said for the retention of old Sanskrit formulae for the most prevalent mantras or verses. That the meaning of them should be properly understood goes without saying.

There can be no fixed rule laid down as to the time devotional acts should take. It depends upon individual temperament. These are precious moments in one's daily life. The exercises are intended to sober and humble us and enable us to realize that nothing happens without his will and that we are but "clay in the hands of the potter." These are moments when one reviews one's immediate past, confesses one's weakness, asks for forgiveness and strength to be and do better. One minute may be enough for some, twenty-four hours may be too little for others.

For those who are filled with the presence of God in them, to labor is to pray. Their life is one continuous prayer or act of worship. For those others who act only to sin, to indulge themselves, and live for self, no time is too much. If they had patience and faith and the will to be pure, they would pray till they feel the definite purifying presence of God within them.

For us ordinary mortals, there must be a middle path between these two extremes. We are not so exalted as to be able to say that all our acts are a dedication, nor perhaps are we so far gone as to be living purely for self. Hence have all religions set apart times for general devotion. Unfortunately these have nowadays become merely mechanical and formal, where they are not hypocritical. What is necessary, therefore, is the correct attitude to accompany these devotions.

For definite personal prayer in the sense of asking God for something, it should certainly be in one's own tongue. Nothing can be grander than to ask God to make us act justly towards everything that lives.

Young India, June 10, 1926

Prayer is nothing else but an intense longing of the heart. You may express yourself through the lips; you may express yourself in the private closet or in public; but to be genuine, the expression must come from the deepest recesses of the heart.

Young India, December 16, 1926

6. True Prayer

True prayer never goes unanswered. It does not mean that every little thing we ask for from God is readily given to us. It is only when we shed our selfishness with a conscious effort and approach God in true humility that our prayers find a response.

In the Ashram Prayer nothing is asked. The prayer is for God to make us better men and women. If the prayer came truly from the heart, God's grace would surely descend upon us. There is not a blade of grass which moves without his will, not one single true thought which does not leave a mark on character. It . is good, therefore, to develop the daily habit of prayer.

Harijan, January 5, 1947

7. True Worship

We have forgotten God and we worship Satan. A man's duty is to worship God. Telling one's beads is no symbol of that worship. Neither is going to mosque or temple, nor saying the *Namaz* [an Islamic prayer] or the *Gayatri*. These things are all right as far as they go. It is necessary to do the one or the other according to one's religion. But by themselves they are no indication of one's being devoted to God in worship. He alone truly adores God who finds his happiness in the happiness of others, speaks evil of none, does not waste his time in the pursuit of riches, does nothing immoral, who acquits himself with others as with a friend, does not fear the plague or any human being.

Collected Works — XI (1964), p. 126

"As is the God, so is the votary," is a maxim worth considering. Its meaning has been distorted and men have gone astray. . . . I am not likely to obtain the result flowing from the worship of God by laying myself prostrate before Satan. If, therefore, anyone were to say, "I want to worship God; it does not matter that I do so by means of Satan," it would be set down as ignorant folly. We reap exactly as we sow.

Hind Swaraj (1962), p. 71

We are all children of the same God. "Verily, verily, I say unto you, not every one that sayeth unto me 'Lord, Lord,' shall enter the Kingdom of Heaven. But he that doeth the will of my Father which is in Heaven shall enter the Kingdom," was said, though in different words, by all the great teachers of the world.

Harijan, April 18, 1936

8. The Greatest Binding Force

Prayer is the greatest binding force, making for the solidarity and oneness of the human family. If a person realizes his unity with God through prayer, he will look upon everybody as himself. There will be no high, no low, no narrow provincialism or petty rivalries in the matter of language between an Andhra and a Tamilian, a Kanarese and a Malayalee. There will be no invidious distinction between a touchable and untouchable, a Hindu and a Musalman, a Parsi, a Christian or a Sikh. Similarly, there would be no scramble for personal gain or power between various groups or between different members within a group.

The outer must reflect the inner. If we are in tune with God, no matter how big a gathering, perfect quiet and order would prevail and even the weakest would enjoy perfect protection. Above all, realization of God must mean freedom from all earthly fear.

Harijan, March 3, 1946

How shall we know [God's] will? By prayer and right living. Indeed prayer should mean right living. There is a *bhajan* [hymn] we sing every day before the Ramayana commences whose refrain is, "Prayer has been never known to have failed anybody. Prayer means being one with God."

Bapu's Letters to Mira, 1924-1948 (1959), p. 286

9. Prayer is All-Inclusive

God does not come down in person to relieve suffering. He works through human agency. Therefore, prayer to God, to enable one to relieve the suffering of others, must mean a longing and readiness on one's part to labor for it.

The prayer is not exclusive. It is not restricted to one's own caste or community. It is all-inclusive. It comprehends the whole of humanity. Its realization would thus mean the establishment of the Kingdom of Heaven on Earth.

Harijan, April 28, 1946

10. A Dialogue With a Buddhist
(By Mahadev Desai)

The Meaning of Prayer

Gandhiji had enough time to think and write during his recent visit to Abottabad, especially as he was kept free of many engagements and interviewers. But even there he had some interviewers — not of the usual type interested in politics or topics of the day, but of the unusual type troubled with ultra-mundane problems. History has it that discourses on such problems used to take place in this region hallowed of old by the steps of the followers of Buddha. One of the interviewers of Gandhiji described himself as a follower of Buddha, and discussed a problem arising out of his creed. He is an archaeologist and loves to live in and dream of the past. Dr. Fabri — for that is his name

— has been in India for many years. He was a pupil of Prof. Sylvan Levy and came out as assistant to the famous archaeologist Sir Aurel Stein. He served in the Archaeological Department for many years, helped in reorganizing the Lahore Museum, and has some archaeological work to his credit. Delving deep in Buddhistic lore has turned him into a stark rationalist. He is a Hungarian and had in the past corresponded with Gandhiji and even sympathetically fasted with him. He had come to Abottabad specially to see Gandhiji.

He was particularly exercised about the form and content of prayer and would very much like to know what kind of prayer Gandhiji said. Could the divine mind be changed by prayer? Could one find it out by prayer?

"It is a difficult thing to explain fully what I do when I pray," said Gandhiji, "but I must try to answer your question. The divine mind is unchangeable, but that divinity is in everyone and everything — animate and inanimate. The meaning of prayer is that I want to evoke that divinity within me. Now I may have that intellectual conviction, but not a living touch. And so when I pray for *swaraj* or independence for India I pray or wish for adequate power to gain that *swaraj* or to make the largest contribution I can towards winning it, and I maintain that I can get that power in answer to prayer."

"Then you are not justified in calling it prayer. To pray means to beg or demand," said Dr. Fabri.

"Yes, indeed. You may say I beg it of myself, of my higher self, the real self with which I have not yet achieved complete identification. You may, therefore, describe it as a continual longing to lose oneself in the divinity which comprises all."

Meditation or Imploration?

"And you use an old form to evoke this?"

"I do. The habit of a lifetime persists, and I would allow it to be said that I pray to an outside power. I am part of that infinite, and yet such an infinitesimal part that I feel outside it. Though I give you the intellectual explanation, I feel, without identification with the divinity, so small that I am nothing. Immediately I begin to say I do this thing and that thing I begin to feel my unworthiness and nothingness, and feel that someone else, some higher power has to help me."

"Tolstoy says the same thing. Prayer really is complete meditation and melting into the higher self, though one occasionally does lapse into imploration like that of a child to his father."

"Pardon me," said Gandhiji, cautioning the Buddhist doctor. "I would not call it a lapse. It is more in the fitness of things to say that I pray to God who exists somewhere up in the clouds, and the more distant he is, the greater is my longing for him and to find myself in his presence in thought. And thought as you know has a greater velocity than light. Therefore, the distance between me and him, though so incalculably great, is obliterated. He is so far and yet so near."

My Prayer Not On a Different Level

"It becomes a matter of belief, but some people like me are cursed with an acute critical faculty," said Dr. Fabri. "For me there is nothing higher than what Buddha taught, and no greater master. For Buddha alone among the teachers of the world said: 'Don't believe implicitly what I say. Don't accept any dogma or any book as infallible.' There is for me no infallible book in the world, inasmuch as all were made by men, however inspired they may have been. I cannot hence believe in a personal idea of God, a Maharaja sitting on the Great White Throne listening to our prayers. I am glad that your prayer is on a different level."

Let it be said in fairness to the savant that he is a devotee of the Bhagavad Gita and the Dhammapada, and those are the two scriptures he carries with him. But he was arguing an extreme intellectual position. Even here Gandhiji caught him from being swept into the torrent of his logic.

"Let me remind you," said Gandhiji, "that you are again only partially true when you say my prayer is on a different level. I told you that the intellectual conviction that I gave you is not eternally present with me. What is present is the intensity of faith whereby I lose myself in an invisible power. And so it is far truer to say that God has done a thing for me than that I did it. So many things have happened in my life for which I had intense longing, but which I could never have achieved myself. And I have always said to my coworkers it was in answer to my prayer. I did not say to them it was in answer to my intellectual effort to lose myself in the divinity in me! The easiest and the correct thing for me was to say, 'God has seen me through my difficulty'."

Karma Alone Powerless

"But that you deserved by your karma. God is justice and not mercy. You are a good man and good things happen to you," contended Dr. Fabri.

"No fear. I am not good enough for things to happen like that. If I went about with that philosophical conception of karma, I should often come a cropper. My karma would not come to my help. Although I believe in the inexorable law of karma I am striving to do so many things, every moment of my life is a strenuous endeavor, which is an attempt to build up more karma, to undo the past and add to the present. It is therefore wrong to say that because my past is good, good is happening at present. The past would be soon exhausted, and I have to build up the future with prayer. I tell you karma alone is powerless. 'Ignite this match,' I say to myself, and yet I cannot if there is no cooperation from without. Before I strike the match my hand is paralyzed or I have only one match and the wind blows it off. Is it an accident or God or higher power? Well, I prefer to use the language of my ancestors or of children. I am no better than a child. We may try to talk learnedly and of books, but when it comes to brass tacks — when we are face to face with a calamity — we behave like children and begin to cry and pray and our intellectual belief gives no satisfaction!"

Did Not Buddha Pray?

"I know very highly developed men to whom belief in God gives incredible comfort and help in the building up of character," said Dr. Fabri. "But there are some great spirits that can do without it. That is what Buddhism has taught me."

"But Buddhism is one long prayer," rejoined Gandhiji.

"Buddha asked everyone to find salvation from himself. He never prayed, he meditated," maintained Dr. Fabri.

"Call it by whatever name you like, it is the same thing. Look at his statues."

"But they are not true to life," said the archaeologist questioning the antiquity of these statues. "They are four hundred years later than his death," said he.

"Well," said Gandhiji, refusing to be beaten by a chronological argument, "give me your own history of Buddha as you may have discovered it. I will prove that he was a praying Buddha. The intellectual conception does not satisfy me. I have not given you a perfect and full definition as you cannot describe your own thought. The very effort to describe is a limitation. It defies analysis and you have nothing but skepticism as the residue."

Be Humble

"What about the people who cannot pray?" asked Dr. Fabri.

"Be humble," said Gandhiji, "I would say to them, and do not limit even the real Buddha by your own conception of Buddha. He could not have ruled the lives of millions of men that he did and does today if he was not humble enough to pray. There is something infinitely higher than intellect that rules us and even the skeptics. Their skepticism and philosophy do not help them in critical periods of their lives. They need something better, something outside them that can sustain them. And so if someone puts a conundrum before me, I say to him, 'You are not going to know the meaning of God or prayer unless you reduce yourself to a cipher.' You must be humble enough to see that in spite of your greatness and gigantic intellect you are but a speck in the universe. A merely intellectual conception of the things of life is not enough. It is the spiritual conception which eludes the intellect, and which alone, can give one satisfaction. Even moneyed men have critical periods in their lives; though they are surrounded by everything that money can buy and affection can give, they find [themselves] at certain moments in their lives utterly distracted. It is in these moments that we have a glimpse of God, a vision of him who is guiding every one of our steps in life. It is prayer."

"You mean what we might call a true religious experience which is stronger than intellectual conception," said Dr. Fabri. "Twice in life I had that experience, but I have since lost it. But I now find great comfort in one or two sayings of Buddha: 'Selfishness is the cause of sorrow,' 'Remember, monks, everything is fleeting.' To think of these takes almost the place of belief."

"That is prayer," repeated Gandhiji with an insistence that could not but have gone home.

Harijan, August 19, 1939

11. Why I Lay Stress on Prayer

I lay stress on prayers because I believe in a higher power. Birth is not just an accident. Each man has to reap the fruits of his karma. Life and death are in God's hands. It would be a good thing if we can think of God throughout the day; but as this is not possible, we should remember him at least for a few minutes daily. If we do not express gratitude for many bounties of providence

daily, life ceases to have any meaning.
Food for the Soul (1957), p. 63

12. Personal Testimony on Prayer

[The following talk on prayer by Gandhiji is reproduced from a letter by Mahadev Desai on his voyage to London.]

But perhaps even a greater center of attraction . . . has been the prayer that we have every evening. The morning prayers are too early to attract these friends, but practically all Indians (who number over forty) — Hindus, Musalmans, Parsis, Sikhs — and a sprinkling of Europeans attend the evening prayers. At the request of some of these friends a fifteen minutes talk after prayer and before dinner has become a daily feature, and I propose to share the first two talks with the readers of *Young India*. A question is asked each evening, and Gandhiji replies to it the next. One of the Indian passengers — a Musalman youth — asked Gandhiji to give his personal testimony on prayer, not theoretical discourse but a narration of what he had felt and experienced as a result of prayer. Gandhiji liked the question immensely, and poured out his personal testimony from a full heart.

"Prayer," said he, "has been the saving of my life. Without it I should have been a lunatic long ago. My autobiography will tell you that I have had my fair share of the bitterest public and private experiences. They threw me into temporary despair. But if I was able to get rid of it, it was because of prayer. Now I may tell you that prayer has not been part of my life in the sense that truth has been. It came out of sheer necessity, as I found myself in a plight when I could not possibly be happy without it. And the more my faith in God increased, the more irresistible became the yearning for prayer. Life seemed to be dull and vacant without it.

"I had attended the Christian service in South Africa, but

it had failed to grip me. I could not join them in prayer. They supplicated God, but I could not do so. I failed egregiously. I started with disbelief in God and prayer and until at a late stage in life I did not feel anything like a void in life. But at that stage I felt that as food was indispensable for the body, so was prayer indispensable for the soul. In fact food for the body is not so necessary as prayer for the soul. For starvation is often necessary in order to keep the body in health, but there is no such thing as prayer-starvation. You cannot possibly have a surfeit of prayer.

"Three of the greatest teachers of the world — Buddha Jesus, Mohammed — have left unimpeachable testimony that they found illumination through prayer and could not possibly live without it. But to come nearer home millions of Hindus and Musalmans and Christians find their only solace in life in prayer. Either you vote them down as liars or self-deluded people. Well, then, I will say that this lying has a charm for me, a truth-seeker, if it is 'lying' that has given me that mainstay or staff of life, without which I could not bear to live for a moment.

"In spite of despair staring me in the face on the political horizon, I have never lost my peace. In fact I have found people who envy my peace. That peace, I tell you, comes from prayer. I am not a man of learning but I humbly claim to be a man of prayer. I am indifferent as to the form. Every one is a law unto himself in that respect. But there are some well-marked roads, and it is safe to walk along the beaten tracks trod by the ancient teachers. Well, I have given my practical testimony. Let every one try and find that as a result of daily prayer he adds something new to his life, something with which nothing can be compared."

"But," said another youth the next evening, "sir, whilst you start with belief in God, we start with unbelief. How are we to pray?"

"Well," said Gandhiji, "it is beyond my power to induce in you a belief in God. There are certain things which are self-proved, and certain which are not proved at all. The existence of

God is like a geometrical axiom. It may be beyond our heart-grasp. I shall not talk of an intellectual grasp. Intellectual attempts are more or less failures, as a rational explanation cannot give you the faith in a living God. For it is a thing beyond the grasp of reason. It transcends reason. There are numerous phenomena from which you can reason out the existence of God, but I shall not insult your intelligence by offering you a rational explanation of that type. I would have you brush aside all rational explanations and begin with a simple childlike faith in God.

"If I exist God exists. With me it is a necessity of my being as it is with millions. They may not be able to talk about it, but from their life you can see that it is part of their life. I am only asking you to restore the belief that has been undermined. In order to do so, you have to unlearn a lot of literature that dazzles your intelligence and throws you off your feet. Start with the faith which is also a token of humility and an admission that we know nothing, that we are less than atoms in this universe. We are less than atoms, I say, because the atom obeys the law of its being, whereas we in the insolence of our ignorance deny the law of nature. But I have no argument to address to those who have no faith.

"Once you accept the existence of God, the necessity for prayers is inescapable. Let us not make the astounding claim that our whole life is a prayer, and therefore, we need not sit down at a particular hour to pray. Even men who were all their time in tune with the infinite did not make such a claim. Their lives were a continuous prayer, and yet for our sake, let us say, they offered prayer at set hours, and renewed each day the oath of loyalty to God. God, of course, never insists on the oath, but we must renew our pledge every day, and I assure you we shall then be free from every imaginable misery in life."

Young India, September 24, 1931

13. Why Pray?

A friend from Baroda writes in English:

"You ask us to pray to God to give light to the whites in South Africa and strength and courage to the Indians there to remain steadfast to the end. A prayer of this nature can only be addressed to a person. If God is an all-pervading and all-powerful force, what is the point of praying to him? He goes on with his work whatever happens."

I have written on this topic before. But as it is a question that crops up again and again in different languages, further elucidation is likely to help someone or the other. In my opinion, Rama, Rahaman, Ahurmazda, God or Krishna are all attempts on the part of man to name that invincible force which is the greatest of all forces.

It is inherent in man, imperfect he though be, ceaselessly to strive after perfection. In the attempt he falls into reverie. And, just as a child tries to stand, falls down again and again and ultimately learns how to walk, even so man, with all his intelligence, is mere infant as compared to the infinite and ageless God. This may appear to be an exaggeration but is not. Man can only describe God in his own poor language. The power we call God defies description. Nor does that power stand in need of any human effort to describe him. It is man who requires the means whereby he can describe that power which is vaster than the ocean.

If this premise is accepted, there is no need to ask why we pray. Man can only conceive God within the limitations of his own mind. If God is vast and boundless as the ocean, how can a tiny drop like man imagine what he is? He can only experience what the ocean is like, if he falls into, and is merged in it. This realization is beyond description. In Madame Blavatsky's language, man, in praying, worships his own glorified self. He can truly pray who has the conviction that God is within him. He who has not, need not pray. God will not be offended, but I can say from experience that he who does not pray is certainly a loser.

What matters then whether one man worships God as a person and another as force? Both do right according to their lights. None knows and perhaps never will know what is absolutely the proper way to pray. The ideal must always remain the ideal. One need only remember that God is the force among all the forces. All other forces are material. But God is the vital force or spirit which is all-pervading, all-embracing and therefore beyond human ken.

Harijan, August 18, 1946

14. The Object of Prayer

The object of prayer is not to please God, who does not want our prayers or praise, but to purify ourselves. The process of self-purification consists in a conscious realization of his presence within us. There is no strength greater than that which such realization gives. Presence of God has to be felt in every walk of life. If you think that as soon as you leave the prayer ground you can live and behave anyhow, your attendance of the prayer is useless.

Harijan, May 26, 1946

Prayer ought to result in self-purification and it ought to transmute our entire conduct. If anybody thinks that it gives him license to do as he likes during the rest of the day, he deceives himself and others. That is a travesty of the true meaning of prayer.

Food for the Soul (1957), p. 80

Prayer does for the purification of the mind what the bucket and the broom do for the cleaning up of our physical surroundings. No matter whether the prayer we recite is the Hindu prayer or the Muslim or the Parsi, its function is essentially the same, namely, purification of the heart.

Food for the Soul (1957), p. 80

15. Spontaneous Upwelling of the Heart

Whatever measure of success I have attained in the realization of truth and nonviolence is the result of prayer.

Prayer should be a spontaneous upwelling of the heart. One should not pray if one feels that the prayer is a burden. God is not hungry for man's prayer or praise. He tolerates all because he is all Love. If we feel that we owe a debt to him, who is the giver of all things, we should remember him and pray to him out of sheer gratitude. The fear of incurring anybody's ridicule or displeasure should never deter one from performing one's elementary duty towards the Maker.

Food for the Soul (1957), p. 62

16. A Man of Prayer Knows No Fear

[On his return from England after the failure of the Round Table Conference, Gandhiji was arrested in Bombay on January 4, 1932 in the quiet of night. Just the day before, at the four o'clock morning prayer, he delivered a stirring message to the people.]

You have been my companions in these prayers for some days, and now that the struggle is resumed again and I may be taken away any moment, I hope you will continue to have your prayers regularly morning and evening. Let it become a daily obligatory ritual for you. Prayer plays a large part in a self-purificatory sacrifice and you will see that it will be a veritable cow of plenty for you, and will make your way clear. The more you apply your-selves to it, the more fearlessness you will experience in daily life, for fearlessness is a sign and symbol of self-purification. I do not know a man or a woman who was on the path of self-puri-fication and was still obsessed by fear.

Generally there are two kinds of fears in men's minds — fear of death and fear of loss of material possessions. A man of prayer and self-purification will shed the fear of death and em-brace death as a boon companion and will regard all earthly possessions as fleeting and of no account. He will see that he has no right to possess wealth when misery and pauperism stalk the land and when there are millions who have to go without a meal. No power on earth can subdue a man who has shed these two fears. But for that purpose the prayer should be a thing of the heart and not a thing of outward demonstration. It must take us daily nearer to God, and a prayerful man is sure to have his heart's desire fulfilled, for the simple reason that he will never have an improper desire. Continue this ritual and you will shed luster not only on your city but on our country. I hope this brief prayer of mine will find a lodgment in your heart.

Young India, January 7, 1932

I am very glad to know that you are not afraid. Why should one fear who knows that God is the protector of all? By saying that God is the protector of all I do not mean that none would be able to rob us or that no animal will attack us. It is no slur on God's protection if such things happen to us — it is only due to our lack of faith in him. The river is forever ready to give water to all. But if one does not go near it with a pot to get water, or avoids it thinking its water poisonous, how can that be the fault of the river?

All fear is a sign of lack of faith. But faith cannot be devel-oped by means of reasoning. It comes gradually through quiet thinking, contemplation and practice. To develop such faith, we pray to God, read good books, seek the company of the good and take to sacrificial spinning at the wheel. He who has no faith will not even touch the spinning-wheel.

Bapu's Letters to Ashram Sisters (1960), p. 28

17. Ramanama: Reciting God's Name

There are many who, whether from mental laziness or from having fallen into a bad habit believe that God is and will help us unasked. Why then is it necessary to recite his name? It is true that if God is, he is irrespective of our belief. But realization of God is infinitely more than mere belief. That can come only by constant practice. This is true of all science. How much more true of the science of all sciences?

Man often repeats the name of God parrot-wise and expects fruit from so doing. The true seeker must have that living faith which will not only dispel the untruth of parrot-wise repetition from within him but also from the hearts of others.

Harijan, May 5, 1946

18. Beauty of Repetition

(By Mahadev Desai)

"This repetition of one and the same thing over and over again jars on me. It may be the defect of my rationalist mathematical temperament. But somehow I cannot like the repetition. For instance, even Bach's wonderful music fails to appeal to me when the text 'Father, forgive them, they know not what they do,' is repeated over and over again."

"But even in mathematics, you have your recurring decimals," said Gandhiji smiling.

"But each recurs with a definite new fact," said the mathematician.

"Even so," said Gandhiji, "each repetition, or *japa* as it is called, has a new meaning, each repetition carries you nearer and nearer to God. This is a concrete fact, and I may tell you that you are here talking to no theorist, but to one who has experienced what he says every minute of his life, so much so that it is easier for the life to stop than for this incessant process to stop. It is definite need of the soul."

"I quite see it, but for the average man it becomes an empty formula."

"I agree, but the best thing is liable to be abused. There is room for any amount of hypocrisy, but even hypocrisy is an ode to virtue. And I know that for ten thousand hypocrites, you would find millions of simple souls who find their solace from it. It is like scaffolding quite essential to a building."

"But," said Pierre Ceresole, "if I may carry the simile a little further, you agree that the scaffolding has to be removed when the building is complete?"

"Yes, it would be removed when this body is removed."

"Why?"

"Because," said Wilkinson who was closely following the discourse, "we are eternally building."

"Because," said Gandhiji, "we are eternally striving after perfection. God alone is perfect, man is never perfect."

Harijan, May 25, 1935

This is how repetition of God's name wipes out one's sins. Anyone who sincerely follows that practice is bound to have faith. He starts with the conviction that such repetition will wipe out his sins. Wiping out of sins means self-purification. One who repeats God's name daily with faith will never grow tired of doing so, and therefore, the name which he repeats with his lips to start with sinks ultimately into his heart, and that purifies him. This is a universal experience. Psychologists also believe that man becomes what he thinks. Ramanama follows this law. I have un-shakable faith in the virtue of repeating God's name. I am con-vinced that the person who discovered it had firsthand experi-ence and that his discovery is of the utmost value. The door of purification should open even for the illiterate. Repetition of God's name opens it for them.

Collected Works — (1972), p. 326

19. No Faith in Prayer

Here is a letter written by a student to the Principal of a na-tional institution, asking to be excused from prayer meetings:

"I beg to state that I have no belief in prayer, as I do not believe in anything known as God to which I should pray. I never feel any necessity of supposing a God for myself. What do I lose if I do not care for him, and calmly and sincerely work my own schemes?

"So far as congregational prayer is concerned, it is of no use. Can such a huge mass of men enter into any mental concen-tration upon a thing, however trifling it may be? Are the little and ignorant children expected to fix their fickle attention on the subtlest ideas of our great scriptures — God, and soul, and equality of all men and many other high-sounding phrases? This great performance is required to be done at a particular time at the command of a particular man. Can love for the so-called Lord take its root in the hearts of boys by any such mechanical function? Nothing can be more repugnant to reason than to expect the same behavior from men of every temperament. There-fore, prayer should not be a compulsion. Let those pray who have a taste for it, and those avoid who dislike it. Anything done without conviction is an immoral, degrading action."

Let us first examine the worth of the last idea. Is it an immoral and degrading act to submit to discipline before one begins to have conviction about its necessity? Is it immoral and degrading to study subjects according to the school syllabus, if one has no conviction about its utility? May a boy be excused from studying his vernacular, if he has persuaded himself that it is useless? Is it not truer to say that a school boy has no conviction about the things he has to learn, or the discipline he has to go through? His choice is exhausted, if he had it, when he elected to belong to an institution. His joining one means that he will willingly submit to its rules and regulations. It is open to him to leave it, but he may not choose what or how he will learn. It is for teachers to make attractive and intelligible, what to the pupils may, at first, appear repulsive or uninteresting.

It is easy enough to say, "I do not believe in God," for God permits all things to be said of him with impunity. He looks at our acts. And any breach of his law carries with it, not its vindictive, but its purifying, compelling, punishment. God's existence cannot be, does not need to be, proved. God is. If he is not felt, so much the worse for us. The absence of feeling is a disease which we shall some day throw off *nolens volens*.

But a boy may not argue. He must, out of sense of discipline, attend prayer meetings if the institution to which he belongs requires such attendance. He may respectfully put his doubts before his teachers. He need not believe what does not appeal to him. But if he has respect for his teachers, he will do without believing what he is asked to do, not out of fear, nor out of churlishness, but with the knowledge that it is right for him so to do, and with the hope that what is dark to him today will some day be made clear to him.

Prayer is not an asking. It is a longing of the soul. It is a daily admission of one's weakness. The tallest among us has a perpetual reminder of his nothingness before death, disease, old age, accidents, etc. We are living in the midst of death. What is the value of working for our own schemes when they might be reduced to naught in the twinkling of an eye, or when we may, equally swiftly and unawares, be taken away from them? But we may feel strong as a rock, if we could truthfully say, "We work for God and his schemes." Then, all is as clear as daylight. Then, nothing perishes. All perishing is, then, only what seems. Death and destruction have then, but only then, no reality about them. For death and destruction is then but a change. An artist destroys his picture for creating a better one. A watchmaker throws away a bad spring to put in a new and a useful one.

A congregational prayer is a mighty thing. What we do not often do alone, we do together. Boys do not need conviction. If they merely attend in obedience to the call to prayer, without inward resistance, they feel the exaltation. But many do not. They are even mischievous. All the same the unconscious effect cannot be resisted. Are there not boys who at the commencement of their career were scoffers, but who subsequently became mighty believers in the efficacy of congregational prayer? It is a common experience for men who have no robust faith to seek the comfort of congregational prayer. All who flock to churches, temples, or mosques are not scoffers or humbugs. They are honest men and women. For them congregational prayer is like a daily bath, a necessity of their existence. These places of worship are not a mere idle superstition to be swept away at the first opportunity. They have survived all attacks up to now, and are likely to persist to the end of time.

Young India, September 23, 1926

A correspondent thus writes on my article "No Faith in Prayer"
"In your article bearing the above caption, you hardly do justice to the 'boy' or to your own position as a great thinker. It is true that the expressions used by the writer in his letter are not all happy, but of his clarity of thought there is no doubt. It is also very evident that he is not a boy as the word is understood. I should be much surprised to find him under twenty. Even if he is young, he seems to show sufficient intellectual development

not to be treated in the manner of 'a boy may not argue.' The writer of the letter is a rationalist while you are a believer, two age-old types with age-old conflict. The attitude of the one is, 'Let me be convinced and I shall believe.' That of the other is, 'Believe and conviction shall come.' The first appeals to reason, the second appeals to authority. You seem to think that agnosticism is but a passing phase among all young people, and that faith comes to them sooner or later. There is the well-known case of Swami Vivekananda to support your view. You, therefore, proceed to prescribe a compulsory dose of prayer to the 'boy' for his own good. Your reasons are twofold. Firstly, prayer for its own sake, as a recognition of one's own littleness, and the mightiness and goodness of the supposed higher being. Secondly, for its utility, for the solace it brings to those who want to be solaced. I shall dispose of the second argument first.

"Here, it is recommended as a sort of staff to the weak. Such are the trials of life, and such is their power to shatter the reason of men, that a great many people may need prayer and faith some time. They have a right to it and they are welcome to it. But there have been, and there are always, some true rationalists — few, no doubt — who have never felt the necessity of either. There is also the class of people who, while they are not aggressive doubters, are indifferent to religion.

"As all people do not ultimately require the help of prayer, and as those who feel its necessity are free to take to it, and do take to it when required, compulsion in prayer, from the point of utility cannot be upheld. Compulsory physical exercise and education may be necessary for physical and mental development of a person, not so the belief in God and prayer for the moral side. Some of the world's greatest agnostics have been the most moral men. To these, I suppose, you would recommend prayer for its own sake, as an expression of humility, in fact, your first argument. Too much has been made of this humility. So vast is knowledge that even the greatest scientists have felt humble sometimes, but their general trait has been that of masterful inquiry. Their faith in their own powers has been as great as their conquest of nature. Had it not been so, we shall still be scratching earth with bare fingers for roots. Nay, we should have been wiped out of the surface of the earth.

"During the Ice Age, when human beings were dying of cold and fire was first discovered, your prototype in that age must have taunted the discoverer with, 'What is the use of your schemes, of what avail are they against the power and wrath of God?' The humble have been promised the Kingdom of God hereafter. We do not know whether they will get it, but here on this earth their portion is serfdom. To revert to the main point, your assertion about 'accept the belief and the faith shall come' is too true, terribly true. Much of the religious fanaticism of this world can be traced directly to this kind of teaching. Provided you catch them young enough, you can make a good majority of human beings believe in anything. That is how your orthodox Hindu, or fanatical Mahomedan, is manufactured. There are, of course, always a small few in either community who will outgrow these beliefs that have been forced upon them. Do you know that if the Hindus and the Mahomedans stopped studying their scriptures until they reached maturity, they would not be such fanatical believers in their dogmas, and would cease to quarrel for their sake? Secular education is the remedy for Hindu-Muslim riots, but you are not made that way.

"Great as our debt is to you for setting an unprecedented example in courage, action and sacrifice in this country where people have been always much afraid, when the final judgment is passed on your work, it will be said that your influence gave a great setback to intellectual progress in this country."

I do not know the meaning of boy "as the word is ordinarily understood," if a twenty-year-old lad is not a boy. Indeed, I would call all school-going persons boys and girls, irrespective of their ages. But whether the doubting student may be called a boy or a man, my arguments must stand. A student is like a soldier (and a soldier may be forty years old) who may not argue about matters of discipline, when he has put himself and chooses to remain under it. A soldier may not remain a unit in his regiment and have the option of doing or not doing things he is asked to do. Similarly, a student, no matter how wise or old he is, surrenders when he joins a school or a college the right of rejecting its discipline. Here, there is no underrating or despising the intelligence of the student. It is an aid to his intelligence for him to come voluntarily under discipline. But my correspondent willingly bears the heavy yoke of the tyranny of words. He scents "compulsion" in every act that displeases the doer. But there is compulsion and compulsion. We call self-imposed compulsion self-restraint. We hug it and grow under it. But compulsion to be shunned, even at the cost of life, is restraint superimposed upon us against our wills, and often with the object of humiliating us and robbing us of our dignity as men and boys, if you will. Social restraints generally are healthy, and we reject them to our own undoing. Submission to crawling orders is unmanly and cowardly. Worse still is the submission to the multitude of passions that crowd round us every moment of our lives, ready to hold us their slaves.

But the correspondent has yet another word that holds him in its chains. It is the mighty word "rationalism." Well, I had a full dose of it. Experience has humbled me enough to let me realize the specific limitations of reason. Just as matter misplaced becomes dirt, reason misused becomes lunacy. If we would but render unto Caesar that which is Caesar's, all would be well.

Rationalists are admirable beings. Rationalism is a hideous monster when it claims for itself omnipotence. Attribution of omnipotence to reason is as bad a piece of idolatry as is worship of stock and stone, believing it to be God.

Who has reasoned out the use of prayer? Its use is felt after practice. Such is the world's testimony. Cardinal Newman never surrendered his reason, but he yielded a better place to prayer when he humbly sang, "One step enough for me." Shankara was a prince among reasoners. There is hardly anything in the world's literature to surpass Shankara's rationalism. But he yielded the first place to prayer and faith.

The correspondent has made a hasty generalization from the fleeting and disturbing events that are happening before us. But everything on this earth lends itself to abuse. It seems to be a law governing everything pertaining to man. No doubt, religion has to answer for some of the most terrible crimes in history. But that is the fault not of religion, but of the ungovernable brute in man. He has not yet shed the effects of his brute ancestry.

I do not know a single rationalist who has never done anything in simple faith, and has based every one of his acts on reason. But we all know millions of human beings living more or less orderly lives because of their childlike faith in the maker of us all. That very faith is a prayer. The "boy" on whose letter I based my article belongs to that vast mass of humanity, and the article was written to steady him and his fellow-searchers, not to disturb the happiness of rationalists like the correspondent.

But he quarrels even with the bent that is given to the youth of the world by their elders and teachers. But that, it seems, is an inseparable handicap (if it be one) of impressionable age. Purely secular education is also an attempt to mold the young mind after a fashion. The correspondent is good enough to grant that the body and the mind may be trained and directed. Of the soul, which makes the body and the mind possible, he has no care or perhaps he is in doubt as to its existence. But this belief cannot avail him. He cannot escape the consequence of his reasoning. For, why may not a believer argue on the correspondent's own ground, and say he must influence the soul of boys and girls, even as the others influence the body and the intelligence? The evils of religious instructions will vanish with the evolution of the true religious spirit. To give up religious instruction is like letting a field lie fallow and grow weeds for want of the tiller's knowledge of the proper use of the field.

The correspondent's excursion into the great discoveries of the ancients is really irrelevant to the subject under discussion. No one questions — I do not — the utility or the brilliance of those discoveries. They were generally a proper field for the use and exercise of reason. But they, the ancients, did not delete from their lives the predominant function of faith and prayer. Works without faith and prayer are like an artificial flower that has no fragrance. I plead not for the suppression of reason, but for a due recognition of that in us which sanctifies reason itself.

Young India, October 10, 1926

20. Why No Faith in Prayer?

And why no faith in prayer? Faith is either derived or revealed from within. You should derive it from the testimony without exception of all the teachers and the seers of all climes, countries and times. A true prayer is not a mere lip expression. It need never lie. Selfless service is prayer. You must not say, "I have no faith in prayer."

Mahadevbhaini Diary, vol. 2 (1949), p. 24

21. Have Faith

Visitor: "If you pray to God, can he intervene and set aside the law for your sake?"

Gandhiji: "God's law remains unaltered, but since that very law says that every action has a result, if a person prays, his prayer is bound to produce an unforeseeable result in terms of his law."

"But do you know the God to whom you pray?'"

"No, I don't."

"To whom shall we pray then?"

"To the God whom we do not know. We do not always know the person to whom we pray."

"Maybe, but the person to whom we pray is knowable."

"So is God. And since he is knowable, we search. It may take a billion years before we find him. What does it matter? So, I say, even if you do not believe, you must continue to pray, i.e., search. 'Help thou my unbelief' is a verse from the Bible to be remembered. But it is not right to ask such questions. You must have infinite patience, and inward longing. Inward longing obviates all such questions. 'Have faith and you will be whole' is another tip from the Bible."

"When I look at nature around me," the venerable visitor finally said, "I say to myself, there must be one Creator, one God, and to him I should pray."

"That again is reasoning," Gandhiji replied. "God is beyond reason. But I have nothing to say if your reason is enough to sustain you."

Mahatma Gandhi, The Last Phase, vol. I (1965), p. 59

I can give you no help if you have no faith in God, and if you have faith in God you need no help from me. Therefore I would advise you to have faith in God and therefore also in prayer. You will then find that all the evil thoughts will leave you and that you will find peace of mind gradually growing on you, and you will become a fit instrument for service.

Collected Works — XLVII (1971), p. 326

22. The Healing Balm

Q: What counsel do you give to the young men who are fighting a losing battle with their lower selves?

A: Simply prayer. One must humble oneself utterly, and look beyond oneself for strength.

Q: But what if the young men complain that their prayer is not heard, that they feel like speaking to brass heavens, as it were?

A: To want an answer to one's prayer is to tempt God. If prayer fails to bring relief it is only lip-prayer. If prayer does not help, nothing else will. One must go on ceaselessly. This, then, is my message to the youth. In spite of themselves, the youth must believe in the all-conquering power of love and truth.

Q: The difficulty with our youth is that the study of science and modern philosophy has demolished their faith, and so they are burnt up by the fire of disbelief.

A: That is due to the fact that with them faith is an effort of the intellect, not an experience of the soul. Intellect takes us along in the battle of life to a certain limit, but at the crucial moment it fails us. Faith transcends reason. It is when the horizon is the darkest and human reason is beaten down to the ground, that faith shines brightest and comes to our rescue. It is such faith that our youth requires, and this comes when one has shed all pride of intellect and surrenders oneself entirely to His will.

Young India, March 21, 1929

23. God's Word

My success lies in my continuous, humble, truthful striving. I know the path. It is straight and narrow. It is like the edge of a sword. I rejoice to walk on it. I weep when I slip. God's word is:

"He who strives never perishes." I have implicit faith in that promise. Though, therefore, from my weakness I fail a thousand times, I will not lose faith, but hope that I shall see the light when the flesh has been brought under perfect subjection, as some day it must.

Young India, June 17, 1926

[I]n all my trials — of a spiritual nature, as a lawyer, in conducting institutions, and in politics — I can say that God saved me. When every hope is gone, "when helpers fail and comforts flee," I find that help arrives somehow, from I know not where. Supplication, worship, prayer are no superstition; they are acts more real than the acts of eating, drinking, sitting or walking. It is no exaggeration to say that they alone are real, all else is unreal.

Such worship or prayer is no flight of eloquency; it is no lip-homage. It springs from the heart. If, therefore, we achieve that purity of the heart when it is "emptied of all but love," if we keep all the chords in proper tune, they "trembling pass in music out of sight." Prayer needs no speech. It is in itself independent of any sensuous effort. I have not the slightest doubt that prayer is an unfailing means of cleansing the heart of passions. But it must be combined with the utmost humility.

Autobiography (1969), p. 54

24. The Only Help of the Helpless

I know from correspondence with the students all over India what wrecks they have become by having stuffed their brains with information derived from a cartload of books. Some have become unhinged, others have become lunatics, some have been leading a life of helpless immaturity. My heart goes out to them when they say that, try as much as they might, they are what they are, because they cannot overpower the devil. "Tell us," they plaintively ask, "how to get rid of the devil, how to get rid of the impurity that has seized us."

When I ask them to take Ramanama and kneel before God and seek his help, they come to me and say, "We do not know where God is. We do not know what it is to pray." That is the state to which they have been reduced. . . .

A Tamil saying has always remained in my memory and it means, "God is the help of the helpless." If you would ask him to help you, you would go to him in all your nakedness, approach him without reservations, also without fear or doubts as to how he can help a fallen being like you. He who has helped millions who have approached him, is he going to desert you? He makes no exceptions whatsoever and you will find that everyone of your prayers will be answered. The prayer of even the most impure will be answered. I am telling this out of my personal experience, I have gone through the purgatory. Seek first the Kingdom of Heaven and everything will be added unto you.

Young India, April 4, 1929

25. God's Covenant

(By Mahadev Desai)
You will wonder why I consented to have a prayer meeting in Bombay when even the existence of God is with many a matter of doubt. There are others who say, "If God is seated in the heart of everyone, who shall pray to whom, who shall invoke whom?" I am not here to solve these intellectual puzzles. I can only say that ever since my childhood prayer has been my solace and my strength. . . .

There are those who are struck with doubt and despair. For them there is the name of God. It is God's covenant that whoever goes to him in weakness and helplessness, him he will make strong. "When I am weak, then I am strong." As the poet

Surdas has sung, Rama is the strength of the weak. His strength is not to be obtained by taking up arms or by similar means. It is to be had by throwing oneself on his name. Rama is but a synonym of God. You may say God or Allah or whatever other name you like, but the moment you trust naught but him, you are strong, all disappointment disappears.

Surdas' hymn alludes to the story of the lord of elephants who was in the jaws of a crocodile and who had been all but drowned in water. There was only the tip of his trunk left above water when he invoked God's name and he was saved. No doubt it is an allegory. But it conceals a truth. Over and over again in my life have I found it. Even in darkest despair, when there seems no helper and no comfort in the wide, wide world his name inspires us with strength and puts all doubts and despair to flight. The sky may be overcast today with clouds, but a fervent prayer to him is enough to dispel them. It is because of prayer that I have known no disappointment. . . . Let us pray that he may cleanse our hearts of pettinesses, meannesses and deceit, and he will surely answer our prayers.

Harijan, June 1, 1935

26. Secret of Self-Control

Moksha is liberation from impure thought. Complete extinction of impure thought is impossible without ceaseless penance. There is only one way to achieve this. The moment an impure thought arises, confront it with a pure one. This is possible only with God's grace, and God's grace comes through ceaseless communion with him and complete self-surrender. This communion may in the beginning be just a lip repetition of his name, even disturbed by impure thoughts. But ultimately what is on the lips will possess the heart. And there is another thing to bear in mind. The mind may wander, but let not the senses wander with it. If the senses wander where the mind takes them, one is done for. But he who keeps control of the physical senses will some day be able to bring impure thoughts under control.

Impure thoughts need not dismay you. We are monarchs of the domain of Effort. God is sole monarch of the domain of Result. . . . You know what to do to create a pure atmosphere about you. Spare diet, sight fixed on the earth below, and impatience with oneself to the extent of plucking the eye out "if it offends thee."

Harijan, February 22, 1942

For me the observance of even bodily *brahmacharya* [chastity; self-control] has been full of difficulties. Today I may say that I feel myself fairly safe, but I have yet to achieve complete mastery over thought, which is so essential. Not that the will or effort is lacking, but it is yet a problem to me wherefrom undesirable thoughts spring their insidious invasions. I have no doubt that there is a key to lock out undesirable thoughts, but every one has to find it out for himself. Saints and seers have left their experiences for us, but they have given us no infallible and universal prescription. For perfection or freedom from error comes only from grace, and so seekers after God have left us mantras, such as Ramanama, hallowed by their own austerities and charged with their purity. Without an unreserved surrender to his grace, complete mastery over thought is impossible. This is the teaching of every great book of religion, and I am realizing the truth of it every moment of my striving after that perfect *brahmacharya*.

Autobiography (1969), p. 238

Prayer and *brahmacharya* are not things of the same kind. *Brahmacharya* is one of the five cardinal vows, and prayer is a means of being able to observe them. I have said a great deal to explain the necessity of *brahmacharya*. But when I tried to think how one can observe it, I discovered a powerful means in prayer. For him

who has realized the value of prayer and is able to pray with concentration, *brahmacharya* becomes quite easy to observe.
Collected Works — L (1972), pp. 377-78

There is however a golden rule for gaining control of the carnal desire. It is the repetition of the divine word "Rama" or such other mantra. Every one must select the mantra after his heart. I have suggested the word "Rama" because I was brought up to repeat it in my childhood and I have ever got strength and sustenance out of it. Whichever mantra is selected, one should be identified with it whilst repeating it. I have not the least doubt of ultimate success as a result of repetition of some such mantra in complete faith, even though other thoughts distract the mind. The mantra will be the light of one's life and will keep one from all distress. Such holy mantras should obviously never be used for material ends. If their use is strictly restricted to the preservation of morals, the results attained will be startling. Of course a mere repetition of such a mantra parrotwise would be of no avail. One should throw his whole soul into it. The parrot repeats it like a machine. We should repeat it with a view to preventing the approach of unwelcome thoughts and with full faith in the efficacy of the mantra to that end.
Young India, June 5, 1924

Real self-control does not come by reading. It comes only by definite realization that God is with us and looks after us as if he had no other care besides. How this happens I do not know. That it does happen I do know. Those who have faith have all their cares lifted off their shoulders. You cannot have faith and tension at the same time.
Bapu's Letters to Mira [1924-1948] (1959), p. 255

27. A Call To Repentance

To err is human. By confessing, we convert our mistakes into stepping stones for advance. On the contrary, a person who tries to hide his mistakes becomes a living fraud and sinks down. Man is neither brute nor God, but a creature of God striving to realize his divinity. Repentance and self-purification are the means. The moment we repent and ask God for forgiveness for our lapse, we are purged of our sin and new life begins for us. True repentance is an essential prerequisite of prayer.

Harijan, April 21, 1946

God does not fail to forgive even those who atone for their sins during the last moments of their life. We must have at heart the welfare of all living beings that exist on the earth, however small or large. To foster this spirit we must daily offer our prayers to the Almighty both in the morning and in the evening. The wishes for the well-being of all also embrace our own welfare.

My Memorable Moments with Bapu (1960), Ch. 25, p. 46

28. Visitations

When a man is down, he prays to God to lift him up. He is the help of the helpless, says a Tamil proverb. The appalling disaster in Quetta [earthquake] paralyses one. It baffles all attempt at reconstruction. The whole truth about the disaster will perhaps never be known. The dead cannot be recalled to life.

Human effort must be there always. Those who are left behind must have help. Such reconstruction as is possible will no doubt be undertaken. All this and much more along the same line can never be a substitute for prayer.

But why pray at all? Does not God, if there be one, know what has happened? Does he stand in need of prayer to enable him to do his duty?

No, God needs no reminder. He is within everyone. Nothing happens without his permission. Our prayer is a heart search. It is a reminder to ourselves that we are helpless without his support. No effort is complete without prayer — without a definite recognition that the best human endeavor is of no effect if it has not God's blessing behind it. Prayer is a call to humility. It is a call to self-purification, to inward search.

I must repeat what I said at the time of the Bihar disaster. There is a divine purpose behind every physical calamity. That perfected science will one day be able to tell us beforehand when earthquakes will occur, as it tells us today of eclipses, is quite possible. It will be another triumph of the human mind. But such triumphs even indefinitely multiplied can bring about no purification of self without which nothing is of any value.

Of course we will forget this latest calamity as we have forgotten the Bihar one. I ask those who appreciate the necessity of inward purification to join in the prayer that we may read the purpose of God behind such visitations, that they may humble us and prepare us to face our maker whenever the call comes, and that we may be ever ready to share the sufferings of our fellows whoever they may be.

Harijan, June 8, 1935

The few lines that I wrote inviting the people to prayer and repentance on the Quetta disaster have given rise to some private correspondence. One of the correspondents asks, "At the time of the Bihar 'quake you had no hesitation in saying that it was to be taken by Savarna Hindus as a fit punishment for the sin of untouchability. For what sin must the more terrible "'quake of Quetta be?" The writer had the right to put the question. What I said about Bihar was deliberately said even as the lines on Quetta were deliberately written.

This call to prayer is a definite yearning of the soul. Prayer is a sign of repentance, a desire to become better, purer. A man of prayer regards what are known as physical calamities as divine chastisement. It is a chastisement alike for individuals and for nations. All chastisements do not equally startle people. Some affect only individuals, some others affect groups or nations only mildly. Disasters like Quetta stun us. Familiarity with ordinary, everyday calamities breeds contempt for them. If earthquakes were a daily occurrence, we would take no notice of them. Even this Quetta one has not caused in us the same disturbance that the Bihar one did.

But it is the universal experience that every calamity brings a sensible man down on his knees. He thinks that it is God's answer to his sins and that he must henceforth behave better. His sins have left him weak, and in his weakness he cries out to God for help. Thus have millions of human beings used their personal calamities for self-improvement. Nations have been known to invoke the assistance of God when calamities have overtaken them. They have abased themselves before God and appointed days of humiliation, prayer and purification.

I have suggested nothing new or original. In these days of fashionable disbelief, it does need some courage to call men and women to repentance. But I can claim no credit for courage, for my weaknesses or idiosyncrasies are well known. If I had known Quetta, as I know Bihar and Biharis, I would certainly have mentioned the sins of Quetta, though they might be no more its specialities than untouchability was Bihar's. But we all — the rulers and the ruled — know that we have many sins personal and national to answer for. The call is to all these to repentance, prayer and purification. True prayer is not a prelude to inaction. It is a spur to ceaseless, selfless action. Purification is never for the selfishly idle, it accrues only to the selflessly industrious.

Harijan, June 15, 1935

Our forefathers and our mothers have taught us to think that, when a calamity descends upon us, it comes because of our personal sin. You know that when rain does not come in time, we perform sacrifices and ask God to forgive us our sins. It is not only here, but I have seen it in England and South Africa that, when locusts descend upon fields or any such thing happens, they appoint days of humiliation, prayer and fasting and pray for the passing of the visitation.

Harijan, February 2, 1934

29. Divine Guidance

(By Mahadev Desai)

Dr. Mott [founder of the Y.M.C.A.]: What has brought deepest satisfaction to your soul in difficulties and doubts and questionings?

Gandhi: Living faith in God.

Dr. Mott: When have you had indubitable manifestation of God in your life and experiences?

Gandhiji: I have seen and believe that God never appears to you in person, but in action which can only account for your deliverance in your darkest hour.

Dr. Mott: You mean things take place that cannot possibly happen apart from God.

Gandhiji: Yes. They happen suddenly and unawares. One experience stands quite distinctly in my memory. It relates to my twenty-one days' fast for the removal of untouchability. I had gone to sleep the night before without the slightest idea of having to declare a fast the next morning. At about twelve o'clock in the night something wakes me up suddenly, and some voice — within or without, I cannot say — whispers "Thou must go on a fast." "How many days?" I ask. The voice again said, "Twenty-one days." "When does it begin?" I ask. It says, "You begin tomorrow." I went quietly off to sleep after making the decision. I did not tell anything to my companions until after the morning prayer. I placed into their hands a slip of paper announcing my decision and asking them not to argue with me, as the decision was irrevocable.

Well, the doctors thought I would not survive the fast but something within me said I would, and that I must go forward. That kind of experience has never in my life happened before or after that date.

Dr. Mott: Now, you surely can't trace such a thing to an evil source?

Gandhi: Surely not. I never have thought it was an error. If ever there was in my life a spiritual fast it was this. There is something in denying satisfaction of the flesh. It is not possible to see God face to face unless you crucify the flesh. It is one thing to do what belongs to it as a temple of God, and it is another to deny it what belongs to it as to the body of flesh.

Harijan, December 10, 1939

In the phrase "seeing God face to face," "face to face" is not to be taken literally. It is a matter of decided feeling. God is formless. He can, therefore, only be seen by spiritual sight-vision.

Mahadevbhaini Diary, vol. I (1948), p. 52

30. Visions

(By Pyarelal)
A professor of Islamia College at Peshawar who came to see Gandhiji during his tour of the Frontier Province asked the latter the question whether he had anything like a prophetic vision. Gandhiji answered him as follows:

"I do not know what you call a vision and what you will call prophetic. But let me give you an experience in my life. When

I announced my fast of twenty-one days in jail I had not reasoned about it. On retiring to bed the previous night I had no notion that I was going to announce the next morning a fast of twenty-one days. But in the middle of the night a voice woke me up and said, 'Go through a fast.' 'How long?' I asked. 'Twenty-one days,' was the answer. Now let me tell you that my mind was unprepared for it, disinclined for it. But the thing came to me as clearly as anything could be.

Let me tell you one thing more and I have done. Whatever striking things I have done in life I have not done prompted by reason but prompted by instinct, I would say God. Take the Dandi Salt March of 1930. I had not the ghost of a suspicion how the breach of the salt law would work itself out. Pandit Motilalji and other friends were fretting and did not know what I would do; and I could tell them nothing, as I myself knew nothing about it. But like a flash it came, and as you know it was enough to shake the country from one end to the other.

One last thing. Until the last day I knew nothing about announcing the sixth of April 1919 as a day of fasting and prayer. But I dreamt about it — there was no voice or vision as in 1930 — and I felt it was just the thing to do. In the morning I shared it with C. R. and announced it to the country, you know with what a wonderfully spontaneous response."

Harijan, May 14, 1938

31. Inner Voice

The "inner voice" is something which cannot be described in words. But sometimes we have a positive feeling that something in us prompts us to do a certain thing. The time when I learnt to recognize this voice was, I may say, the time when I started praying regularly. That is, it was about 1906. I searched my memory and tell you this because you asked the question. In fact, however, there was no moment when I suddenly felt that I had some new experience. I think my spiritual life has grown without my being conscious of the fact in the same way as hair grows on our body.

Collected Works — L (1972), p. 326

There is something within me impelling me to cry out my agony. I have known exactly what to do. That something which never deceives me tells me now, "You have to stand against the whole world although you may have to stand alone. You have to stare the world in the face although the world may look at you with bloodshot eyes. Do not fear. Trust that little thing in you which resides in the heart and says, "Forsake friends, wife, all; but testify to that for which you have lived and for which you have to die."

Homage to the Departed (1958), p. 202

Q: Does the "Inner Voice" mean the "message of God"?

A: The "Inner Voice" may mean a message from God or the Devil, for both are wrestling in the human breast. Acts determine the nature of the voice.

Young India, February 13, 1930

No act of mine is done without prayer. Man is a fallible being. He can never be sure of his steps. What he may regard as an answer to prayer, may be an echo of his pride. For infallible guidance, man has to have a perfectly innocent heart incapable of evil. I can lay no such claim. Mine is a struggling, striving, erring, imperfect soul. But I can rise only by experimenting upon myself and others.

Young India, September 15, 1924

Part II.
Forms and Methods
of Prayer

32. *Yajna* (Sacrifice)

Now to offer prayers is easy enough. But they are not heard unless they are offered from a pure and contrite heart. Let me tell you that *yajna* has a deeper meaning than the offering of ghee [clarified butter] and other things in the sacrificial fire. *Yajna* is sacrifice of one's all for the good of humanity. . . . We have to offer up our weaknesses, our passions, our narrowness into the purifying fire so that we may be cleansed. Then and then only our prayers would be heard.

Let me also place before you another aspect of prayer. You have assembled here for the fulfillment of your desires, and the *yajna* is performed to that purpose. Now desires may be good and bad, and not every one of us knows which of his desires is good and pure and which not. It is he who presides over our thoughts and acts who knows this, and so I always pray that God may grant only such of my desires as may be good and pure, and reject all my prayers if they partake of impurity or grossness. I invite you to join me in that kind of prayer today.

One last thing. The prayer for peace is accepted on all hands as a pure prayer, and in these times of severe strife and cruel bloodshed it is well that we offer prayers for peace. There is a great Vedic prayer which I should like to recite in this connection, and I am sure you will all join me when I do so:

Whatever is heinous, and cruel and sinful,

may all that be stilled;
may everything be good and peaceful for us.

Harijan, May 3, 1942

33. How I Establish Communion With God

I do not know whether I am a *karmayogi* or any other *yogi*. I know that I cannot live without work. I crave to die with my hand at the spinning wheel. If one has to establish communion with God through some means, why not through the spinning wheel? "Him who worships me," says the Lord in the Gita, "I guide along the right path and set to his needs." My God is myriad-formed, and while sometimes I see him in the spinning wheel, at other times I see him in communal unity, then again in removal of untouchability; and that is how I establish communion with him according as the spirit moves me.

Harijan, May 8, 1937

34. The Form of My Prayer

(By Pyarelal)
A missionary who called on Gandhiji at his retreat in Segaon asked him, "What is your method of worship?"

In reply, Gandhiji said, "We have joint worship morning and evening at 4:20 A.M. and 7 P.M. This has gone on for years. We have a recitation of verses from the Gita and other accepted religious books, also hymns of saints with or without music. Individual worship cannot be described in words. It goes on continuously and even unconsciously. There is not a moment when I do not feel the presence of a witness whose eye misses nothing and with whom I strive to keep in tune. I do not pray as Christian friends do. Not because I think there is anything wrong in it, but because words won't come to me. I suppose it is a matter of habit."

Missionary: Is there any place for supplication in your prayer?

Gandhiji: There is and there is not. God knows and anticipates our wants. The deity does not need my supplication, but I, a very imperfect human being, do need his protection as a child that of its father. And yet I know that nothing I do is going to change his plans. You may call me a fatalist, if you like.

Missionary Do you find any response to your prayer?

Gandhiji: I consider myself a happy man in that respect. I have never found him lacking in response. I have found him nearest at hand when the horizon seemed darkest — in my ordeals in jails when it was not all smooth sailing for me. I cannot recall a moment in my life when I had a sense of desertion by God.

Harijan, December 24, 1938

1. When I pray, I do not ask for anything but I simply think of some of the verses or hymns which I fancy for the moment.

2. The relation between God and myself is not only at prayer but, at all times, that of master and slave in perpetual bondage.

3. Prayer is to me the intense longing of the heart to merge myself in the master. If a man does not pray, evidently he has no longing; there is no feeling of helplessness and when there is no helplessness, there is no need for help.

Collected Works — XXXI (1969), p. 542

35. Service is Prayer

If I found myself entirely absorbed in the service of the community, the reason behind it was my desire for self-realization. I had made the religion of service my own, as I felt that God could be realized only through service. And service for me was the service of India, because it came to me without my seeking, because I had an aptitude for it. I had gone to South Africa for travel, for finding an escape from Kathiawad intrigues and for gaining my own livelihood. But as I have said, I found myself in search of God and striving for self-realization.

An Autobiography (1969), p. 118

What I want to achieve — what I have been striving and pining to achieve these thirty years — is self-realization, to see God face to face, to attain *moksha* [liberation]. I live and move and have my being in pursuit of this goal. All that I do by way of speaking and writing, and all my ventures in the political field, are directed to this same end.

An Autobiography, Introduction, p. x

I never asked my audience to substitute the spinning wheel for the rosary. I only suggested that they could go on spinning taking the name of Narayana [God] simultaneously. And whilst today the whole country is on fire, I think it behooves us all to fill the buckets of the spinning wheel with the water of yarn and extinguish the fire with the name of Narayana on our lips.

✿   ✿   ✿

Narasimha Mehta does indeed sing the praise of the rosary, and the praise is well-merited where it is given. But the same Narasimha has sung:

Of what avail is the rosary and the muttering of the Name, of what avail is the grammatical interpretation of the Veda, what avail is the mastery of the letters? All these are devices to fill the belly and nothing worth without their helping to a realization of the Para-Brahma.

The Musalman does count the beads of his *tasbih*, and the Christian of the rosary. But both would think themselves fallen from religion if their *tasbih* and rosary prevented them from running to the succor of one who, for instance, was lying stricken with a snakebite. Mere knowledge of the Vedas cannot make our Brahmanas spiritual preceptors. If it did, Max Müller would have become one. The Brahmana who has understood the religion of today will certainly give Vedic learning a secondary place and propagate the religion of the spinning wheel, relieve the hunger of the millions of his starving countrymen, and only then, and not until then, lose himself in Vedic studies. . . .

I certainly did not repeat the divine word "Rama," nor count the beads on account of a feeling that my end was near. But I was too weak then to turn the wheel. I do count the rosary whenever it helps me in concentrating on Rama. When, however, I rise to a pitch of concentration where the rosary is more a hindrance than a help, I drop it. If it was possible for me to turn the wheel in my bed, and if I felt that it would help me in concentrating my mind on God, I would certainly leave the rosary aside and turn the wheel. If I am strong enough to turn the wheel, and I have to make a choice between counting beads or turning the wheel, I would certainly decide in favor of the wheel, making it my rosary, so long as I found poverty and starvation stalking the land. I do look forward to a time when even repeating the name of Rama will become a hindrance. When I have realized that Rama transcends even speech, I shall have no need to repeat the name. The spinning wheel, the rosary and the Ramanama are all the same to me. They serve the same end, they teach me the religion of service.

Young India, August 14, 1924

In my opinion, God's name and God's work go hand in hand. There is no question of preference because the two are indivisible. A parrot-like repetition of the name is worse than useless, and service or action without the consciousness that it is done in God's name and for God's sake is also valueless. And if we sometimes pass our time in merely repeating the name of the deity as we have to, it is simply a course of preparation for self-dedication, that is, service for the sake of and in the name of God, and when we are thoroughly attuned, continued service in that spirit is itself equal to the repetition of the name of the deity. In the vast majority of cases, however, the setting apart a part of our time for prayer is a vital necessity.

Collected Works — XXIII (1967), p. 289

Devotion to duty is itself prayer. We go and pray in order to be qualified for doing actual service. But when one is engaged in actual practice of duty, prayer is merged with the execution of duty. If someone who is engaged in deep prayer, hears the cry of another who is stung by a scorpion, she is bound to leave the prayer and run to help him. Prayer finds fulfillment in the service of the distressed.

Bapu's Letters to the Ashram Sisters (1960), p. 79

The real way to pray to Lord Krishna is to do in his name some little service to those who are less fortunate than ourselves.

Mahadevbhaini Diary, vol. 2 (1949), p. 243

There is no worship purer or more pleasing to God than selfless service of the poor. The rich in their arrogance and intellectual pride often forget God and even question his existence. But God dwells among the poor as they cling to him as their sole refuge and shelter. To serve the poor is therefore to serve him.

Young India, February 14, 1929

Q: Would it not be better for a man to give the time he spends on the worship of God to the service of the poor? should not true service make devotional worship unnecessary for such a man?

A: I sense mental laziness as also agnosticism in this question. The biggest of *karmayogis* never give up devotional song or worship. Idealistically it may be said that true service of others is itself worship and that such devotees do not need to spend any time in songs, etc. As a matter of fact, *bhajans* etc. are a help to true service and keep the remembrance of God fresh in the heart of the devotee.

Harijan, October 13, 1946

36. Thy Will Be Done

There is really only one prayer that we may offer: "Thy will be done." Some one will ask where is the sense in offering such a prayer. The answer is: Prayer should not be understood in a gross sense. We are aware of the presence of God in our heart, and in order to shake off attachment, we for the moment think of God as different from ourselves and pray to him. That is to say, we do not wish to go where our wayward will may lead us but where the Lord takes us. We do not know whether it is good to live or to die. Therefore we should not take delight in living, nor should we tremble at the thought of death. We should be equiminded towards both. This is the ideal. It may be long before we reach it, and only a few of us can attain it. Even then we must keep it constantly in view, and the more difficult it seems of attainment, the greater should be the effort we put forth.

The Diary of Mahadev Desai, vol. I (1953), pp. 118-19

(By Kakasaheb Kalelkar)
It was when Bapu was translating the *Ashram Bhajanavali* [collection of devotional songs sung at the ashram prayers] into English for the benefit of Mirabehn. He set aside a little time daily after prayers for this task and, soon, his translation was complete. There is one verse which runs, "Victory, victory to thee,

Oh Shri Mahadeva Shambho, Ocean of Mercy!"

I have both read and made English translations of Sanskrit verses. "Jaya, jaya" simply means "victory, victory". But Bapu had translated it, "Thy will be done." "How is this, Bapu?" I asked. He replied, "The Lord is ever victorious throughout his creation. We pray that lust, anger, etc., which are for ever becoming victorious in our hearts, might be conquered and rendered impotent; that they might be routed. In other words, we pray that we might be enabled to do all things in accordance with the will of God. For a Christian, the best rendering of this can only be 'Thy Kingdom come,' or 'Thy will be done'. After all, what do we pray for? Is it not simply that God should be ever victorious in our own hearts?"

Stray Glimpses of Bapu (1960), p. 159

37. Resign to His Will

A prayer can be offered in connection with some person or thing, and may even be granted. But if it is offered without any such specific end in view, it will confer a greater benefit on the world as well as ourselves. Prayer exerts an influence over ourselves; our soul becomes more vigilant, and the greater its vigilance, the wider the sphere of its influence.

Prayer is a function of the heart. We speak aloud in order to wake it up. The power that pervades the universe is also present in the human heart. The body does not offer it any obstruction. The obstruction is something of our own making, and is removed by prayer. We can never know if a prayer has or has not yielded the desired result. I may pray for Narmada's relief from pain. Even if she is free from pain afterwards, I must not assume that that is due to my prayer.

Prayer is never fruitless, but we cannot know what the fruit of it is. Nor should we imagine that it is a good thing if it yields the desired result. Here too the Gita doctrine has to be practiced. We may pray for something and yet remain free from attachment. We may pray for some one's *mukti* [salvation] but should not worry whether he gets or does not get what we want for him. Even if the result is just the opposite of what we had asked for, that is no reason for the conclusion that the prayer has been fruitless.

The Diary of Mahadev Desai, vol. I (1953), p. 233

(By Pyarelal)
Commenting on the allegory of Gajendra and Graha, the elephant king and the alligator that adorns the Bhagawata, Gandhiji remarked, "The moral of the story is that God never fails his devotees in the hour of trial. The condition is that there must be a living faith in and the uttermost reliance on him. The test of faith is that having done our duty we must be prepared to welcome whatever he may send — joy as well as sorrow, good luck as well as bad. . . .

"A man of prayer will in the first place be spared mishaps by the ever merciful Providence, but if the mishaps do come he will not bewail his fate but bear it with an undisturbed peace of mind and joyous resignation to his will."

Harijan, July 7, 1946

God is the hardest taskmaster I have known on this earth, and he tries you through and through. And when you find that your faith is failing you, and you are sinking, he comes to your assistance somehow or other and proves to you that you must not lose your faith and that he is always at your beck and call, but on his terms, not on your terms. So I have found. I cannot really recall a single instance when at the eleventh hour, he has forsaken me.

Speeches and Writings of Mahatma Gandhi, p. 1066

38. How and To Whom To Pray

"Often, sir, do you ask us to worship God, to pray, but never tell us how to and to whom to do so. Will you kindly enlighten me?" asks a reader of *Navajivan*.

Worshipping God is singing the praise of God. Prayer is a confession of one's unworthiness and weakness. God has a thousand names or rather, he is nameless. We may worship or pray to him by whichever name that pleases us. Some call him Rama, some Krishna, others call him Rahim, and yet others call him God. All worship the same spirit, but as all foods do not agree with all, all names do not appeal to all. Each chooses the name according to his associations, and he being the In-Dweller, All-Powerful and Omniscient knows our innermost feelings and responds to us according to our deserts.

Worship or prayer, therefore, is not to be performed with the lips, but with the heart. And that is why it can be performed equally by the dumb and the stammerer, by the ignorant and the stupid. And the prayers of those whose tongues are nectared but whose hearts are full of poison are never heard. He, therefore, who would pray to God, must cleanse his heart. Rama was not only on the lips of Hanuman. He was enthroned in his heart. He gave Hanuman exhaustless strength. In his strength he lifted the mountain and crossed the ocean. It is faith that steers us through stormy seas, faith that moves mountains and faith that jumps across the ocean. That faith is nothing but a living, wide awake consciousness of God within. He who has achieved that faith wants nothing. Bodily diseased he is spiritually healthy; physically pure, he rolls in spiritual riches.

"But how is the heart to be cleansed to this extent?" one might well ask. The language of the lips is easily taught but who can teach the language of the heart? Only the *bhakta* — the true devotee — knows it and can teach it. The Gita has defined the *bhakta* in three places, and talked of him generally everywhere.

But a knowledge of the definition of a *bhakta* is hardly a suffi-cient guide. They are rare on this earth. I have, therefore, sug-gested the religion of service as the means. God of himself seeks for his seat the heart of him who serves his fellow men. That is why Narasimha Mehta who "saw and knew" sang, "He is a true Vaishnava who knows how to melt at other's woe." Such was Abu Ben Adhem. He served his fellow men, and therefore, his name topped the list of those who served God.

But who are the suffering and the woebegone? The sup-pressed and the poverty-stricken. He who would be a *bhakta*, there-fore, must serve these by body, soul and mind. How can he who regards the "suppressed" classes as untouchables serve them by the body? He who does not even condescend to exert his body to the extent of spinning for the sake of the poor and trots out lame excuses does not know the meaning of service. An able-bodied wretch deserves no alms, but an appeal to work for his bread. Alms debase him. He who spins before the poor inviting them to do likewise serves God as no one else does. "He who gives me even a trifle as a fruit or a flower or even a leaf in the spirit of *bhakti* is my servant," says the Lord in the Bhagavadgita. As he hath his footstool where live "the humble, the lowliest and lost," spinning, therefore, for such is the greatest prayer, the great-est worship, the greatest sacrifice.

Prayer, therefore, may be done by any name. A prayerful heart is the vehicle and service makes the heart prayerful. Those Hindus who in this age serve the untouchables from a full heart truly pray; the Hindus and those others who spin prayerfully for the poor and the indigent truly pray.

Young India, September 24, 1925

A correspondent writes:

"You say that the rule should be that during prayers, every-one should sit with closed eyes and think of nothing but God. The question arises as to how and in what form we have to think of God?"

True meditation consists in closing the eyes and ears of the mind to all else except the object of one's devotion. Hence the closing of eyes during prayers is an aid to such concentration. Man's conception of God is naturally limited. Each one has, therefore, to think of him as best appeals to him, provided that the conception is pure and uplifting.

Harijan, August 18, 1946

Prayer brings a peace, a strength and a consolation that nothing else can give. But it must be offered from the heart. When it is not offered from the heart, it is like the beating of a drum, or just the vocal effect of the throat sounds. When it is offered from the heart, it has the power to melt mountains of misery. Those who want are welcome to try its power.

Young India, December 19, 1927

A person must shed all spiritual dirt at prayer time. As he is ashamed of doing anything immoral while other people are looking on, so should he be in the presence of God. But God knows our every act and every thought. There is not a single moment when we can think any thought or do any act unknown to him. He who thus prays from the bottom of his heart will in time be filled with the spirit of God and become sinless.

The Diary of Mahadev Desai, vol. I (1953, pp. 232-33)

39. Punctuality at Prayers

(By Kakasaheb Kalelkar)
It must have been during Bapu's tour of South Bharat in September 1927. The Tamilnad tour had ended, and we were covering Andhra by car. We reached Chikakol at about 10 P.M., and found that the local workers had organized a spinning competi-

tion between the best women spinners there, in Bapu's honor. Chikakol *khadi* [handspun cloth] is famous throughout the length and breadth of Bharat for its remarkable fineness and beauty. We were dead tired with all the night-and-day traveling in a motorcar, and in no mood for any programs or competitions. Mahadevbhai and I thought, "Poor Bapu can't get out of this competition, but why shouldn't we? It won't make any difference to anybody whether we go or not. Much better to snatch a little sleep when one can!" So Mahadevbhai and I went off to our sleeping places and fell fast asleep. Bapuji's bed had been prepared for him. We never knew when he came.

We rose at 4 A.M. for prayers. We washed our faces and were just beginning the prayers when Bapu asked, "Did you say your prayers before sleeping last night?" I replied, "I was so tired when I came to bed that I just went off to sleep, clean forgetting my prayers. I remember it just this moment, when you ask us about it."

Mahadevbhai said, "It was the same with me, but just as I was dropping off, I remembered that we had not prayed, so I sat up in bed and rectified the omission. I did not wake Kaka, though."

Then Bapu said, with indescribable pathos, "I sat for an hour or so in the competition, and when I returned, I was so tired that I, too, forgot all about prayer and went to sleep. Then, at about two o'clock, I woke up, and it flashed upon me that I had not said my nightly prayers. I felt such agony that my body was seized with a fit of trembling, and I became all wet with perspiration. I sat up in bed, and was plunged in a remorse beyond all description. How could I forget him by whose mercy I live, who strengthens me in all my efforts? How could I forget that Bhagavan? I could not get over my own carelessness. I could not sleep a wink after that. All night I sat up in bed, repenting my mistake and begging his forgiveness."

Saying this he became silent. It may be imagined with what

feelings we said our morning prayers that day. Mahadevbhai sang a *bhajan* [hymn]. Then Bapu said, "Even while traveling, we must have a fixed time for our evening prayers. We make a mistake in leaving our prayers till we have finished all our work and are preparing to go to bed. From today, we pray punctually at seven o'clock in the evening, no matter where we may happen to be."

We were still journeying by car. Every evening at seven o'clock, we would stop the car, and, whether we were in a forest or in a town, we would say our prayers without fail, at the appointed time.

Stray Glimpses of Bapu (1960), pp. 112-14

40. God's Time Never Stops

It should be the general rule that prayers must not be delayed for anybody on earth. God's time never stops. As a matter of fact, there is no beginning for him or his time. . . . How can anyone afford to miss the time of offering prayers to him, whose watch never stops?

Harijan, June 16, 1946

[Uttered on the way to the prayer-ground on the fateful evening of January 30, 1948]
I do not like being late for the prayers. . . . Even a minute's delay for the prayer causes me great discomfort.

The End of An Epoch (1962), p. 41

41. Never Miss Prayers

It is five minutes to seven. So you must now be on your way to the prayer-ground. You must keep to whatever time you might fix. I take it that all those who promised to attend prayers are

attending them, except for reasons quite beyond their control.
Bapu's Letters to Ashram Sisters (1960), p. 3

There should be no break in the prayers. Never mind if [they are offered] late. It would be better if it is not late. Even if it is late it should not be that the prayers are not offered. Food can be given up but not the prayers.
Collected Works — L (1972), pp. 133-34

I once saw a beautiful painting in a Roman Catholic Church, the work of a gifted painter. It is the time of prayer. Women have been working in the fields, pick axes in hand. As one of them was about to dig, her pickax fell from her hand, she bent her body and started praying. The poet — for the painter is a poet — had imagined the woman as working like a machine. For these women work was worship. There is a saying in Latin which means that bodily labor is a form of worship. Anyone who believes that it is so will automatically kneel down at prayer time. A person who has resolved that he will always get up at four will roll up his bed as the clock, strikes four. If such a person misses praying at prayer time, he will feel weary and oppressed and will not be able to concentrate on any work.
Collected Works — XXXII (1969), p. 201

One must never forget prayer. As the body craves for food when it is hungry and does not forget about it, so the soul should yearn to pray, The prayer may consist of nothing more than Ramanama, but one ought not to forget it in any circumstances. To the extent that you forget it occasionally, to that extent it is an external thing to you. Prayer must become so intimately a part of one's being that at last one's every breath is accompanied by Ramanama. As an eyelid goes on doing its work, one will go on repeating Rama's name with every breath.
Collected Works — XLIX (1972), p. 71

42. Attendance at Prayers

I hear that attendance at prayers is again becoming thinner. It should not be necessary for me to explain at this hour of the day that no one should expect someone else to stimulate his or her interest in prayers. The interest should be felt within. As the body needs food and feels hungry, so the soul needs and feels hungry for prayer. Prayer is a form of communication with God. So long as our need for attendance at prayers is not the same as that for attendance at meals, for which we require no one to goad us, so long our faith in God is weak; or, though we sub-scribe to the rules of the ashram, we do not observe them and to that extent we are unfaithful to it and violate the vow of truth. Anyone who realizes this will not remain absent at prayers — whether morning or evening — without some strong reason.
Collected Works — XXXVIII (1970), p. 197

If we strive for truth, we would not be content merely to attend prayers but would try to concentrate our attention on them. We would try to follow the songs and the discourses, be punctual in attending the prayers and respond to them as to a fresh experi-ence every day. The freshness does not consist in the variety of *bhajans* or other recitations, but should result from the increasing purity of our heart. We should grow daily more contented and feel greater peace of mind. If we do not have this experience, the fault will lie not with the quality of the prayers, but with the element of untruthfulness in us. If we attend the prayers with sincere devotion to truth, we would experience nothing but peace.

The faithful who visit temples do not observe the lack of cleanliness in them, or pay attention to the hypocrisy of the priest. They do not see the image as a stone. They experience peace in the midst of noise and return from the temples purified in heart. A person like me who feels suffocated by the noise there and sees the image only as a piece of stone should never visit a temple. God appears to us in the form in which we worship him. For he is not outside of us. He is in the hearts of us all. If we understand this truth, our simplest and smallest actions would shed luster on us and help us to see God. In order that we may learn this, prayers, spinning and other daily duties are like a spiritual lighthouse to us or a right angle which is the standard of measurement.

Collected Works — XLV (1971), pp. 21-22

You ought to get up in time and attend prayers every day. You may excuse yourselves from other duties, but never from prayers. You should cultivate such a state of mind that for half an hour you will have only one thought in your mind, and no other. Everyone should set apart time in this manner for reflection. It provides an opportunity to feel one with all living creatures.

Collected Works — XXXII (1969), p. 220

As I have already said, you have come to the ashram not to lose your Christianity, but to perfect it.

If you don't feel the presence of God at the prayer meetings then remember that the names Rama and Krishna signify the same as Jesus to you.

You should most decidedly not attend these meetings. You should go and pray in your private chamber. The prayer meetings are not meant to force anyone into a position. They are meant for free men and women. The children must attend. Those who abstain from sheer laziness must attend. But for you, no one can misunderstand your abstinence. You will therefore please do that which gives you the greatest peace. The ashram is nothing if it does not enable you to realize God more and more fully day by day.

My Dear Child (1959), pp. 45-46

43. The Spiritual Value of Silence

It has often occurred to me that a seeker after truth has to be silent. I know the wonderful efficacy of silence. I visited a Trappist monastery in South Africa. A beautiful place it was. Most of the inmates of that place were under a vow of silence. I inquired of the Father the motive of it and he said the motive is apparent. "We are frail human beings. We do not know very often what we say. If we want to listen to the still small voice that is always speaking within us, it will not be heard if we continually speak." I understood that precious lesson. I know the secret of silence.

Young India, August 6, 1925

Silence is a part of the spiritual discipline of a votary of truth. Proneness to exaggerate, to suppress or modify the truth, wittingly or unwittingly, is a natural weakness of man, and silence is necessary in order to surmount it.

A man of few words will rarely be thoughtless in his speech; he will measure every word. We find so many people impatient to talk. There is no chairman of a meeting who is not pestered with notes for permission to speak. And whenever the permission is given the speaker generally exceeds the time limit, asks for more time, and keeps on talking without permission. All this talking can hardly be said to be of any benefit to the world. It is so much waste of time.

Autobiography (1969), p. 46

When one comes to think of it one cannot help feeling that nearly half the misery of the world would disappear if we, fretting mortals, knew the virtue of silence. Before modern civilization came upon us, at least six to eight hours of silence out of twenty-four were vouchsafed to us. Modern civilization has taught us to convert night into day and golden silence into brazen din and noise. What a great thing it would be if we in our busy lives could retire into ourselves each day for at least a couple of hours and prepare our minds to listen in to the voice of the great silence. The divine radio is always singing if we could only make ourselves ready to listen to it, but it is impossible to listen in without silence. St. Theresa has used a charming image to sum up the sweet result of silence.

"You will at once feel your senses gather themselves together; they seem like bees which return to the hive and there shut themselves up to work at the making of honey; and this will take place without effort or care on your part. God thus rewards the violence which your soul has been doing to itself, and gives to it such a domination over the senses that a sign is enough, when it desires to recollect itself, for them to obey and so gather themselves together. At the first call of the will they come back more and more quickly. At last after many and many exercises of this kind, God disposes them to a state of absolute repose and of perfect contemplation."

Harijan, September 24, 1938

Silence is a great help to a seeker after truth like myself. In the attitude of silence the soul finds the path in a clearer light, and what is elusive and deceptive resolves itself into crystal clearness. Our life is a long and arduous quest after truth, and the soul requires inward restfulness to attain its full height.

Truth is God (1959), p. 53

(By Mahadev Desai)
Dr. Mott concluded his visit in 1936 with a question on silence. He had done so during a brief flying visit to Ahmedabad in 1928 and during this visit too he asked if Gandhiji had continued to find it necessary in his spiritual quest.

Gandhiji: I can say that I am an everlastingly silent man now. Only a little while ago I have remained completely silent nearly two months and the spell of that silence has not yet broken. I broke it today when you came. Nowadays I go into silence at prayer time every evening and break it for visitors at 2 o'clock. I broke it today when you came. It has now become both a physical and spiritual necessity for me. Originally it was taken to relieve the sense of pressure. Then I wanted time for writing. After, however, I had practiced it for some time I saw the spiritual value of it. It suddenly flashed across my mind that that was the time when I could best hold communion with God. And now I feel as though I was naturally built for silence. Of course I may tell you that from my childhood I have been noted for my silence. I was silent at school, and in my London days I was taken for a silent drone by friends.

Dr. Mott: In this connection you put me in mind of two texts from the Bible:

"My soul, be thou silent unto God."
"Speak Lord, for thy servant hearkeneth."
Harijan, December 10, 1938

44. Blind Penance

(By Mahadev Desai)
A dear friend and keen seeker after truth who has gone through several fasts and has long been on a pilgrimage of search, meeting sadhus and mortifying the flesh, has written saying that he has now taken a twelve years' silence; that, not content with this, he proposes to have his lips sewn up with thin wire and that off and on he takes a fortnight's fast and now practically lives on raw flour soaked in water! Here is Gandhiji's reply:

"I was delighted to have your letter after months, but I was pained also. I hold that the remedies you are adopting for self-realization are not right. Silence of the sewn-up lips is no silence. One may achieve the same result by chopping off one's tongue, but that too would not be silence. He is truly silent who, having the capacity to speak, utters no idle word. The penance you are going through is the *tamasi tapas* — blind penance — described in the Gita. Eating raw flour is against all dietetic rules, and certainly not enjoined by religion. If you must have uncooked food, you can live on fruits and nuts. You may add milk to it and that will make an ideal dietary. I wish you could shake yourself free of this self-torture. Ponder over Kabir's song:

"Oh, good man, natural communion is best. Ever since by the grace of God it was achieved, it has been growing. Wherever I wander it is a circuit round the deity. Whatever I do is an act of service. Every lying down of mine is an act of prostration before God. Every utterance of mine is God's name. I worship no other God, and all hearing is a remembrance of God. Eating and drinking are acts of worship, and living in a house or in the wilderness are the same to me. I shut not my eyes neither do I stuff my ears; to no torture do I subject myself. I open my eyes to find nothing but the beautiful manifestation of God here to greet and delight me. My mind ever intent on him, all corrupt thought has left me. So very much I am engrossed in contemplation of him that there is no room in me for aught else. Kabir says: This is a state to be silently enjoyed but I have dared to sing about it. It is a state beyond misery and bliss. I am merged in it."

Harijan, June 24, 1933

45. Communion of Silence

(By Pyarelal)
Last week I referred to the Sunday silent prayer meeting of the Quakers which Gandhiji attended. He has been attending it every Sunday since his arrival here [in Delhi].

Quakers believe that "in corporate silent waiting, God does speak to us and we can understand His will in the common walks of life." As Shri Ranjit M. Chetsingh explained at the beginning of the service last week quoting an early Quaker, "The thinking busy soul excludes the voice of God. Be still and cool from thine own self." Said George Fox, "The silence of a religious and spiritual worship is not a drowsy unthinking state of mind but a withdrawing of it from all visible objects and vain imaginings."

Making the Quaker meeting which he had attended the theme of his address at the evening prayer gathering, Gandhiji described how his own experience tallied with that of the Quakers. "Emptying of the mind of all conscious processes of thought and filling it with the spirit of God unmanifest brings one ineffable peace and attunes the soul with the infinite."

The question may however be raised, should not one's whole life be an unbroken hymn of praise and prayer to the maker? Why then have a separate time for prayer at all? Brother Lawrence testified that "with him the set times of prayers were not different from other times; that he retired to pray according to the directions of his superior, but that he did not want such retirement, nor asked for it, because his greatest business did not divert him from God." Gandhiji does not question that view. "I agree " he observed in his discourse, "that if a man could practice the presence of God all the twenty-four hours, there would be no need for a separate time for prayer." But most people find that impossible. The sordid everyday world is too much with them. For them the practice of complete withdrawal of the mind from all outward things, even though it might be only for a few minutes every day, would be found to be of infinite use. Silent communion would help them to experience an undisturbed peace in the midst of turmoil, to curb anger and cultivate patience.

"When the mind is completely filled with His spirit one cannot harbor ill-will or hatred towards any one and reciprocally the enemy will shed his enmity and become a friend. It is not my claim that I have always succeeded in converting enemies into friends, but in numerous cases it has been my experience that when the mind is filled with His peace all hatred ceases. An unbroken succession of world teachers since the beginning of time has borne testimony to the same. I claim no merit for it. I know it is due entirely to God's grace. Let us then in the sacred week seek his grace through the communion of silence and maybe the experience will abide with us forever afterwards."

Harijan, April 28, 1946

46. Silent Prayers

As I believe the silent prayer is often mightier than any overt act in my helplessness, I continuously pray in the faith that the prayer of a pure heart never goes unanswered. And, with all the strength at my command, I try to become a pure instrument for acceptable prayer.

Young India, September 22, 1927

My faith is increasing in the efficacy of silent prayer. It is by itself an act — perhaps the highest act, requiring the most refined diligence.

Harijan, November 5, 1938

I greatly admire these silent prayers. We must devote a part of our time to such prayers. They afford peace of mind. I have experienced this in my own life. Notwithstanding my manifold activities, I devote as much time as possible to prayer.

Food for the Soul (1957), p. 35

A silent prayer is often more effective than the spoken word consciously uttered.

Collected Works — XXXVIII (1970), p. 281

Peace and order are necessary at all gatherings, but are specially so at prayer gatherings. People come together for prayers in order to obtain peace, to hear God's name and to recite it. Therefore, those who come should really attune themselves even at the start from their homes. Let them be silent and let their thoughts dwell as they walk, on prayer. Otherwise coming to prayer was useless.

Harijan, May 19, 1946

47. Silence During Prayers

Five minutes' silence during the evening prayer was suggested by me. It would be better to have the same period of silence in the morning also. If the congregation has its heart in the matter, all sounds must cease by and by. Even the children would learn to cooperate. I have attended meetings where silence was observed for half an hour in England. . . . It is true that when we practice silence at first, many thoughts enter our minds and we even begin to doze. Silence is intended to remedy these defects.

We are accustomed to talk much and hear loud sounds. Silence therefore seems difficult. A little practice however enables us to like it, and when we like it it gives us a sense of ineffable peace. We are seekers of truth. We must therefore understand what silence means and observe it accordingly. We can certainly take Ramanama during silence. The fact is that we should prepare the mind for it. We shall realize its value if we bestow a little thought on it.

Can we not sit steadily in the congregation for five minutes? Have you ever been at a dramatic performance? Talking is prohibited in many theaters. Enthusiasts like myself will be there an hour before the play begins. In their enthusiasm they do not mind being silent for that hour. But that is not all. The play takes four or five hours, during which the spectator has to observe silence. But he likes it all the same. The silence is not burdensome to him because his mind is attuned to it. Why then can we not be silent for five minutes for God's sake? If there is a flaw in this argument, do let me know. But if it is sound, keep silence with interest and plead on my behalf with those who are opposed to it.

The Diary of Mahadev Desai, vol. I (1953), pp. 312-13.

(By Pyarelal)
"True culture requires that there should be perfect peace in the prayer ground at the time of the prayer." There should be an atmosphere of solemnity as in a church, a mosque or a temple. [Gandhiji] knew that many of the temples were full of clamor. It had hurt him deeply. "We go to the temple to worship not the stone or the metal image, but God who resides in it. The image becomes what man makes of it. It has no power independently of the sanctity with which it is invested by the worshipper. Therefore everyone, including children, should observe perfect silence at the time of prayer."

Harijan, April 28, 1946

48. How I Introduced Congregational Prayer

I introduced the practice of having congregational prayer some time before the commencement of the South African Satyagraha struggle. The Indian community there was faced with a grave peril. We did all that was humanly possible. All methods of seeking redress, agitation through the press and the platform, petitions and deputations, were tried out but proved of no avail. What was the Indian community, consisting of a mere handful of illiterate, indentured labourers mostly, with a sprinkling of free merchants, hawkers, etc., to do in the midst of an overwhelming majority of negroes and whites ? The whites were fully armed. It was clear that if the Indians were to come into their own, they must forge a weapon which would be different from and infinitely superior to the force which the white settlers commanded in such ample measure. It was then that I introduced congregational prayer in Phoenix and Tolstoy Farm as a means for training in the use of the weapon of Satyagraha or soul force.

The singing of *Ramadhun* is the most important part of congregational prayer. The millions may find it difficult to correctly recite and understand the Gita verses and the Arabic and Zend Avesta prayers, but everybody can join in chanting Ramanama or God's name. It is as simple as it is effe:ctive. Only it must proceed from the heart. In its simplicity lies its greatness and the secret of its universality. Anything that millions can do together becomes charged with a unique power.

Harijan, April 7, 1946

49. Congregational Prayer

It becomes a man to remember his maker all the twenty-four hours. If that cannot be done we should at least congregate at prayer time to renew our covenant with God. Whether we are Hindus or Musalmans, Parsis, Christians or Sikhs, we all worship the same God. Congregational prayer is a means for establishing the essential human unity through common worship. Mass singing of Ramadhun and the beating of *tal* are its outward expression. If they are not a mechanical performance but are an echo of the inner unison, as they should be, they generate a power and an atmosphere of sweetness and fragrance which has only to be seen to be realized.

Harijan, March 3, 1946

For me [prayer] has been both a joy, and a privilege, in as much as I have felt its elevating influence. I ask you to keep it up. You may not know the verses, you may not know Sanskrit and the hymns, but Ramanama is there for all, the heritage handed down from ages. And I tell you why I ask you to continue this congregational prayer. Man is both an individual and a social being. As an individual he may have his prayer during all the waking hours, but as a member of society he has to join in the congregational prayer.

I for one may tell you that when I am alone I do have my prayer, but I do feel very lonely without a congregation to share the prayer with me. I knew and even now know very few of you, but the fact that I had the evening prayers with you was enough for me. Among the many memories that will abide in my heart after I leave Bangalore, not the least will be the prayer meetings. But I shall have my congregation at the next place I reach, and forget the wrench. For one who accepts the brotherhood of man and fatherhood of God, should find a congregation wherever he goes, and he may not hug or nurse the feeling of parting or separation.

Please, therefore, keep up the prayer. You can form your own congregation in your own places, and as a last resource one's family can become one's congregation well enough. Do meet every evening at this hour, learn a few hymns, learn the Gita, do the best and the most you can for the purpose of self-purification.

Young India, September 8, 1927

Q: You believe in mass prayer. Is congregational worship as practised today a true prayer? In my opinion, it is a degrading thing and therefore dangerous. Jesus said, "When thou prayest, thou shalt not be as the hypocrites are, but enter into thine inner chamber and having shut thy door pray to the Father which is in secret." Most people in a crowd are inattentive and unable to concentrate. Prayer then becomes hypocrisy. The *yogi* is aware of this. Should not the masses, therefore, be taught self-examination, which is the true prayer?

A: I hold that congregational worship held by me is true prayer for a collection of men. The convener is a believer and no hypocrite. If he were one, the prayer would be tainted at the source. The men and women who attend do not go to any orthodox prayer from which they might have to gain an earthly end. The bulk of them have no contact with the convener. Hence it is presumed, they do not come for show. They join in because they believe that they somehow or other acquire merit by having common prayer. That most or some persons are inattentive or unable to concentrate, is very true. That merely shows that they are beginners. Neither inattention nor inability to concentrate are any proof of hypocrisy or falsity. It would be if they pretended to be attentive when they were not. On the contrary, many have often asked me what they should do when they are unable to concentrate.

The saying of Jesus quoted in the question is wholly inapplicable. Jesus was referring to individual prayer and to hypocrisy underlying it. There is nothing in the verse quoted against collective prayer. I have remarked often enough that without individual prayer, collective prayer is not of much use. I hold that individual prayer is a prelude to collective, as the latter, when it is effective, must lead to the individual. In other words, when a man has got to the stage of heart prayer, he prays always, whether in the secret or in the multitude.

I do not know what the questioner's *yogi* does or does not. I know that the masses, when they are in tune with the infinite, naturally resort to self-examination. All real prayer must have that end.

Harijan, September 22, 1946

50. Cooperative Prayer

The object of our attending prayers is to commune with God

and turn the searchlight inwards so that, with God's help, we can overcome our weaknesses.

I believe that one imbibes pure thought in the company of the pure. Even if there is only one pure man, the rest would be affected by that one man's purity. The condition is that we attend the prayers with that intention, otherwise our coming to the prayers is meaningless.

I go further and maintain that even if we all had our weaknesses but came to the prayer meeting with the intention of removing them, our collective effort made from day to day would quicken the progress of reform. For, even as co-operation in the economic or political field is necessary, so is co-operation much more necessary on the moral plane. That is the meaning of the prayer meetings which I have been holding since my return to India.

I, therefore, appeal to you to sit absolutely quiet with your eyes closed, so as to shut yourselves off from outside thoughts for a few minutes at least. This cooperative prayer needs no fasts, no advertisement. It must be free from hypocrisy.

Food for the Soul (1957), pp. 63-64

51. My Faith in Public Prayer

Speaking for myself, I can say that I can do, and have often done, without food for days on end, but I cannot do without prayers even for a single day. Individual prayer is there, but no one should fight shy of collective prayer. Man is a social being. If men and women can eat together, play together and work together, why should they not pray together? Why should anyone feel the need to pray away from everybody's gaze? Is there anything sinful or shameful in prayer that it should not be said in public?

Crowds Attend My Prayers

For close on fifty years, I have been a believer in public prayer. From my earliest days in South Africa, I had among my associates and co-workers men and women of every religion — Hindus, Muslims, Christians and Parsis — who all used to join me in the prayer. In India, men and women in crowds attend my prayers wherever I go. I have been told that one reason why people feel no interest in community prayers may be that they do not come to attend the prayers; they come just to have my *darshan* [to be in the presence of a holy man]. Even if it is so they come because they want to join me — a man of prayer.

Food for the Soul (1957), pp. 61-62

52. Individual Prayer

Though I have already written once on this subject, I feel that I should again write something about its importance. It seems to me that they do not realize the necessity of individual prayer. The idea of community prayers arose from the individual's need for prayer. If individuals do not feel such a need, how can a community? Community prayers also are for the benefit of individuals. They help people in their effort to attain knowledge of the self — for self-purification. It is, therefore, necessary that all of us should understand the importance of individual prayer. As soon as a child learns to understand things, its mother ought to teach it to pray. This practice is common to all religions.

There are at least two clear times for such prayer. That is, we should turn our mind to the Lord within immediately on awakening in the morning and when closing our eyes for sleep in the evening. During the rest of the day, every man and woman who is spiritually awake will think of God when doing anything and do that with him as witness. Such a person will never do anything evil, and a time will come when he or she will think every thought with God as witness and as its master. This will be a state in which one will have reduced oneself to a cipher. Such a person, who lives constantly in the sight of God, will every moment feel Rama dwelling in his heart.

For such prayers, no special mantra or *bhajan* is necessary. Though generally a mantra is recited at the commencement and conclusion of every religious act, that is not at all necessary. We have only to turn our thoughts to God, no matter by what name we call him, by what method and in what condition. Very few form such a habit. If most people followed this practice, there would be less sin and evil in this world, and our dealings with one another would be pure. In order that we may attain such a pure state, every body should pray at least at the two times which I have mentioned. Each person may fix other hours, too, according to his convenience, and gradually increase their frequency so that, ultimately, his every breath will be accompanied with Ramanama.

Such individual prayer consumes no time at all. It requires not time but wakefulness. As we don't feel that the unceasing action of blinking consumes any time so also we do not feel that praying inwardly does. But we are aware that the eyelids are doing their work; similarly prayer should go on constantly in our heart. Anybody who wishes to pray in this manner should know that he cannot do it with an impure heart. He must, therefore, banish all impurity from his heart when praying. As one feels ashamed of doing anything wicked when being observed by somebody, so also should one feel ashamed of acting similarly in the sight of God. But God watches every action and knows every thought of ours. Hence there can be no moment when we can do anything or think any thought unobserved by him. Thus, anybody who prays to God with his heart will, in the end, become filled with him and so become sinless.

Collected Works — L (1972), pp. 245-46

I can easily understand your prefering group prayer, for you started praying in that manner. But you must also pray by yourself, even if it be only for one minute. Our aspiration should be that ultimately we shall continually and silently go on repeating God's name in our heart, and that is impossible unless one forms the habit of praying by oneself.

Collected Works — L (1972), p. 136

Individual prayer alone can be the basis of congregational prayer. My emphasis on the latter does not at all mean that I attach greater importance to it. Since we are not used to congregational prayer, I have attempted to show the need for it. What you can experience in seclusion is certainly difficult, if not impossible, to experience in a group. I have also noticed that some people cannot pray except in a group. For such people individual prayer is essential. I would also admit that one can do without congregational prayer, but certainly not without individual prayer.

Collected Works — LI (1972), p. 304

53. Concentration During Prayers

Q: Is it possible during prayers (for thousands assemble at your prayer gatherings) to concentrate their minds on anything whatever?

A: I can only answer yes. For if I did not believe in mass prayer, I should cease to hold public prayers. My experience confirms my belief. Success depends upon the purity of the leader and the faith of the audience. I know instances in which the audience had faith and the leader was an impostor. Such cases will continue to happen. But truth like the sun shines in the midst of the darkness of untruth. The result in my case will be known probably after my death.

Even if your mind wanders when praying, you should keep

up the practice. You should retire to a secluded spot, sit in the correct posture and try to keep out all thoughts. Even if they continue to come, you should nevertheless complete the prayer. Gradually the mind will come under control. The Gita also says that the mind is restless, but it tells us that with patient effort we can bring it under control. "We shall never willingly accept defeat, though we lose our life in the struggle."

Collected Works — XLIX (1972), p. 446

54. Compulsory Prayer

Q: I am a worker in the Rajasthan branch of the A.I.S.A. I believe in prayer but some of my colleagues do not. Still they have got to join in prayer under the rules of the Sanstha. They are afraid that, if they refuse, they would lose their job. My view is that the Sanstha pays wages to its workers for their eight hours' work. What right has it to insist upon including compulsory participation in prayer by their workers into the bargain.

A: There can be no such thing as compulsory prayer. A prayer to be prayer must be voluntary. But nowadays people entertain curious ideas about compulsions. Thus, if the rules of your institution require every inmate — paid or unpaid — to attend common prayer, in my opinion you are bound to attend it as you are to attend to your other duties. Your joining the institution was a voluntary act. You knew or ought to have known its rules. Therefore, your attendance at prayer I would regard as a voluntary act, even as I would treat your other work under the contract. If you joined the institution merely because of the wages it offered, you should have made it clear to the manager that you could not attend prayer. If in spite of your objection you entered the institution without stating your objection, you did a wrong thing for which you should make expiation. This can be done in two ways — by joining the prayer with your heart in it, or by resigning and paying such compensation as may be necessary for the loss caused by your sudden resignation. Everyone joining an institution owes it to obey the rules framed by the management from time to time. When any new rule is found irksome, it is open to the objector to leave the institution in accordance with the provisions made for resignation. But he may not disobey them whilst he is in it.

Harijan, July 13, 1940

55. The Malady of Intolerance

The prayer meeting began today as usual. When the verses from the Koran were being recited a member of the audience objected to the recitation. He was arrested by the policeman but Gandhiji immediately stopped the prayer, and requested the policeman who had arrested him to set him free. He would be ashamed to pray, he said, where a man had been arrested for doing what he had done. . . .

Another person was arrested a little later when he took exception to the recitation of Koranic verses during the prayers and shouted, *"Hindu Dharmaki Jay."* Gandhiji then discontinued the prayers.

Gandhiji requested the police to set the man free as it put him [Gandhiji] to shame if anybody was arrested for objecting to what he did.

Gandhiji deplored such narrow-mindedness on the part of the people. Mere shouting of slogans would not carry Hinduism anywhere, he said. He was at a loss to understand why some Hindus objected to his reading the Koran verses in his prayer. If at places the Muslims had not behaved as they should, then it did not mean that the Hindus should retaliate by opposing the reading of the Koran.

The verse from the Koran that was being recited, Gandhiji

said, was a mighty prayer in praise of God. How did it harm the Hindu religion if the prayer was recited in the Arabic language? He who said so knew neither his religion nor his duty. That prayer could also be recited in a temple.

Harijan, May 11, 1947

56. A Word to Objectors

As one person in the audience objected to the *Al Fateha* [a Moslem prayer] being recited, prayers were not held on the Birla House lawn. Gandhiji, however, addressed the audience. He said that he was not going to argue with the objector. He realized the anger that raged in people's hearts today. The atmosphere was so surcharged that he thought it right to respect even one objector, but this by no means meant that he gave up God or his worship in his heart. Prayer demanded a pure atmosphere. One thing that everyone should take to heart from such objections was that those who were anxious to serve must have endless patience and tolerance. One must never seek to impose one's views on others.

☆   ☆   ☆

Though I believe that I was wise in having yielded to a solitary objector and refrained from holding public prayer, it is not improper to examine the incident a little more fully. The prayer was public only in the sense that no member of the public was debarred from attending it. It was on private premises. Propriety required that those only should attend who believed wholeheartedly in the prayer including verses from the Koran. Indeed the rule should be applicable to prayer held even on public grounds. A prayer meeting is not a debating assembly. It is possible to conceive prayer meetings of many communities on the same plot of land. Decency requires that those who are opposed to particular prayers would abstain from attending the meetings they object to. The reverse would make any meeting impossible without disturbance. Freedom of worship, even of public speech, would become a farce if interference became the order of the day. In decent society the exercise of this elementary right should not need the protection of the bayonet. It should command universal acceptance.

Harijan, May 10, 1947

57. Fasting and Prayer

Fasting is an institution as old as Adam. It has been resorted to for self-purification, or for some ends noble as well as ignoble. Buddha, Jesus and Mohammed fasted so as to see God face to face. Ramchandra fasted for the sea to give way for his army of monkeys. Parvati fasted to secure Mahadev himself as her lord and master. In my fasts I have but followed these great examples, no doubt for ends much less noble than theirs.

*   *   *

We have it in our shastras that whenever things go wrong, good people and sages go in for *tapasya*, otherwise known as austerities. Gautama himself, when he saw oppression, injustice and death around him, and when he saw darkness in front of him, at the back of him, and each side of him, went out in the wilderness and remained there fasting and praying in search of light. And if such penance was necessary for him who was infinitely greater than all of us put together, how much more necessary is it for us?

Young India, April 18, 1929

My religion teaches me that whenever there is distress which one cannot remove, one must fast and pray.
Young India, September 25, 1924

I know now more fully than ever that there is no prayer without fasting, be the latter ever so little. And this fasting relates not merely to the palate, but all the senses and organs. Complete absorption in prayer must mean complete exclusion of physical activities till prayer possesses the whole of our being and we rise superior to, and are completely detached from, all physical functions. That state can only be reached after continual and voluntary crucifixion of the flesh. Thus all fasting, if it is a spiritual act, is an intense prayer or a preparation for it. It is a yearning of the soul to merge in the divine essence.
Harijan, July 8, 1933

The prayer is not vain repetition nor fasting mere starvation of the body. Prayer has to come from the heart which knows God by faith, and fasting in abstinence from evil or injurious thought, activity or food. Starvation of the body when the mind thinks of a multiplicity of dishes is worse than useless.
Harijan, April 10, 1937

While appealing to people to fast and pray during the National Week, Gandhiji wrote:

"A genuine fast cleanses body, mind and soul. It crucifies the flesh and to that extent sets the soul free. A sincere prayer can work wonders. It is an intense longing of the soul for its even greater purity. Purity thus gained when it is utilized for a noble purpose becomes a prayer. The mundane use of the *Gayatri* [ancient prayer to the sun god], its repetition for healing the sick, illustrates the meaning we have given to prayer. When the same *Gayatri Japa* is performed with a humble and concentrated mind in an intelligent manner in times of national difficulties and calamities, it becomes a most potent instrument for warding off danger, There can be no greater mistake than to suppose that the recitation of the *Gayatri*, the *Namaz* or the Christian prayer are superstitions fit to be practised by the ignorant and the credulous.

Fasting and prayer therefore are a most powerful process of purification and that which purifies necessarily enables us the better to do our duty and to attain our goal. If therefore fasting and prayer seem at times not to answer, it is not because there is nothing in them but because the right spirit is not behind them.

A man who fasts and gambles away the whole of the day as do so many on Janmashtami Day, naturally, not only obtains no result from the fast in the shape of greater purity, but such a dissolute fast leaves him, on the contrary, degraded. A fast to be true must be accompanied by a readiness to receive pure thoughts and determination to resist all Satan's temptations. Similarly, a prayer to be true has to be intelligible and definite. One has to identify oneself with it. Counting beads with the name of Allah on one's lips, whilst the mind wanders in all directions, is worse than useless.

Young India, March 24, 1920

Prayer expresses the soul's longing and fasting sets the soul free for efficacious prayer.

✳   ✳   ✳

I would urge the modern generation not to regard fasting and prayer with scepticism. The greatest teachers of the world have derived extraordinary powers for the good of humanity and attained clarity of vision through fasting and prayer. Much of this discipline runs to waste because instead of being a matter of the heart, it is often resorted to for stage effect.

Collected Works — XVI (1965), p. 207

It is my conviction and my experience that, if fasting and prayer are done with a sincere heart and in a religious spirit, marvelous results could be obtained from them. There is nothing as purifying as a fast, but fasting without prayer is barren; it may result in a diseased person being restored to health or may only mean a healthy person suffering unnecessarily. A fast undertaken purely for ostentation or to inflict pain on others is a sin. Hence, it is only a prayerful fast undertaken by way of penance to produce some effect on oneself which can be called a religious fast.

Collected Works — XVI (1965), pp. 230, 231

58. The Truest Prayer

There is no prayer without fasting, taking fasting in its widest sense. A complete fast is a complete and literal denial of self. It is the truest prayer. "Take my life and let it be, always only all for thee" is not, should not be, a mere lip or figurative expression. It has to be a reckless and joyous giving without the least reservation. Abstention from food and even water is but the mere beginning, the least part of the surrender.

Whilst I was putting together my thoughts for this article, a pamphlet written by Christians came into my hands wherein was a chapter on the necessity of example rather than precept. In this occurs a quotation from the third chapter of Jonah. The prophet had foretold that Nineveh, the great city, was to be destroyed on the fortieth day of his entering it:

"So the people of Nineveh believed God, and proclaimed a fast, and put on sack-cloth, from the greatest of them even to the least of them. For word came unto the King of Nineveh, and he arose from his throne and he laid his robe from him and covered him with a sack-doth, and sat in ashes. And he caused it to be proclaimed and published through Nineveh by the decree of the king and the nobles saying, 'Let neither man nor beast, herd nor flock, taste anything; let them not feed, nor drink water. But let man and beast be covered with sack-cloth and cry mightily unto God. Yea, let them turn everyone from his evil way, and from the violence that is in their hands. Who can tell if God will turn and repent, and turn away from his fierce enger, that we perish not?' And God saw their works, that they turned from their evil way, and God repented of the evil that he had said that he would do unto them, and he did it not."

Thus this was a "fast unto death." But every fast unto death is not suicide. This fast of the king and the people of Nineveh was a great and humble prayer to God for deliverance. It was to be either deliverance or death. This chapter from the book of Jonah reads like an incident in the Ramayana.

Harijan, April 15, 1933

The shastras tell us that when people in distress prayed to God for relief and he seemed to have hardened his heart, they declared a "fast unto death" till God had listened to their prayer. Religious history tells us of those who survived their fast because God listened to them, but it tells us nothing of those who silently and heroically perished in the attempt to win the answer from a deaf God.

I am certain that many have died in that heroic manner, but without their faith in God and nonviolence being in the slightest degree diminished. God does not always answer prayers in the manner we want him to. For him life and death are one, and who is able to deny that all that is pure and good in the world persists because of the silent death of thousands of unknown heroes and heroines!

Harijan, March 4, 1933

59. The Inner Meaning of the Fast

My religion says that only he who is prepared to suffer can pray to God. Fasting and prayer are common injunctions in my religion. But I know of this sort of penance even in Islam. In the life of the Prophet, I have read that the Prophet often fasted and prayed and forbade others to copy him. Someone asked him why he did not allow others to do the thing he himself was doing. "Because I live on food divine," he said. He achieved most of his great things by fasting and prayer.

I learnt from him that only he can fast who has inexhaustible faith in God. The Prophet had revelations not in moments of ease and luxurious living. He fasted and prayed, kept awake for nights together and would be on his feet at all hours of the night as he received the revelations. Even at this moment, I see before me the picture of the Prophet thus fasting and praying. It is my own firm belief that the strength of the soul grows in proportion as you subdue the flesh.

Young India, October 23, 1924

Under certain circumstances [fasting] is the one weapon which God has given us for use in times of utter helplessness. We do not know its use or fancy that it begins and ends with mere deprivation of physical food. It is nothing of the kind. Absence of food is in indispensable but not the largest part of it. The largest part is prayer — communion with God. It more than adequately replaces physical food.

Bapu's Letters to Mira ⌊1924-1918⌋ (1959), p. 251

It was only when in terms of human effort that I had exhausted all resources and realized my utter helplessness, that I laid my head in God's lap. That is the inner meaning and significance of my fast. You would do well to read and ponder over *Gajendra Moksha*, the greatest of devotional poems as I have called it. Then alone perhaps will you be able to appreciate the step I have taken. *The End of an Epoch* (1962), p. 25

60. Gita, The Mother

The Gita is the universal mother. She turns away nobody. Her door is wide open to any one who knocks. A true votary of the Gita does not know what disappointment is; he ever dwells in perennial joy and peace that passeth understanding. But that peace and joy come not to the skeptic nor to him who is proud of his intellect or learning. It is reserved only for the humble in spirit who brings to her worship a fullness of faith and an undivided singleness of mind. There never was a man who worshipped her in that spirit and went back disappointed.

Our students are prone to be upset by trifles. A trivial thing like failure in an examination plunges them into the darkest despair. The Gita inculcates upon them the duty of perseverance in the face of seeming failure. It teaches us that we have a right to actions only but not to the fruit thereof, and that success and failure are one and the same thing at bottom. It calls upon us to dedicate ourselves, body, mind and soul, to pure duty, and not to become mental voluptuaries at the mercy of all chance desires and undisciplined impulses. As a Satyagrahi, I can declare that the Gita is ever presenting me with fresh lessons. If somebody tells me that this is my delusion, my reply to him would be that I shall hug this delusion as my richest treasure.

I would advise the students to begin their day with an early morning recitation of the Gita. I am a lover and devotee of Tulasidas. I adore the great spirit that gave to an aching world the all-healing mantra of Ramanama. But I am here today not to present Tulasidas to you, but to ask you to take up the study of the Gita, not in a carping or critical spirit, but in a devout and reverent spirit. Thus approached, she will grant your every wish.

It is no joke, I admit, remembering by heart all the eighteen chapters, but it is worthwhile to make the attempt. Once you have tasted of its sweet nectar, your attachment to it will grow from day to day. The recitation of the Gita verses will support you in your trials and console you in your distress, even in the darkness of solitary confinement. And, if with these verses on your lips you receive the final summons and deliver up your spirit, you will attain Brahma-Nirvan — the final Liberation.

Harijan, August 24, 1934

61. The Meditation of Mother Gita

(By Mahadev Desai)
In a letter to Bhau, Bapu gave detailed instructions about *dhyana* [meditation]:

"There is nothing wrong if you draw a picture by your own imagination and meditate over it. But nothing like it if one could rest content with the meditation of Mother Gita. This can be done either by thinking of one's dead mother as the Symbol of the Gita or by drawing a self-imagined, mental picture. ... The second method is preferable if possible. We may meditate on any Gita verse or even one single word in it. Every word in the Gita is an ornament of hers, and to think of an ornament of our beloved object is as good as thinking of it itself. But some one could devise a third mode of meditation and should be free to practise his own device. Every brain works differently from every other brain. No two persons think of the same thing in the same way. There is bound to be some difference or other between their descriptions and imaginings.

"As the sixth chapter assures us, the least little *sadhana* [spiritual effort] is not wasted. The seeker will proceed further in his next birth, starting from it as a base. Similarly if a person has the will but not the ability to make spiritual progress, his environment in his subsequent birth will be such as to strengthen that will. But this fact must not be made an excuse for relaxation now. If it is so made, it means that the will is only intellectual and not heartfelt. Intellectual willing serves no useful purpose, as it does not persist after death. If the will is heartfelt, it must manifest itself in effort. But it is quite possible that physical weakness as well as the environment may come in its way. Even so, when the soul leaves the body, it carries its goodwill with it, which fructifies into deed in the subsequent birth when circumstances are more favourable. Thus one who does good is sure to make steady progress.

"Jnaneshvar may have meditated on Nivritti during the latter's lifetime. But we must not follow his example. One on whom we meditate must be a perfect individual. To ascribe such perfection to a living person is improper and unnecessary."

The Diary of Mahadev Desai, vol. I (1953), pp. 170-72

62. The Use of Images in Prayer

I do not forbid the use of images in prayer. I only prefer the worship of the formless. This preference is perhaps improper. One thing suits one man, another thing will suit another man, and no comparison can fairly be made between the two.

You are not right about Shankara and Ramanuja. Spiritual experience has greater influence than environment. The seeker of truth should not be affected by his surroundings but rise above them. Views based on the environment are often found to be wrong. For instance take the case of body and soul. The soul being at present in close contact with the body, we cannot at once realize her as distinct from her physical venture. Therefore it was a very great man indeed who rose above his environment and said, "It (the soul) is not this (the body)." The language of saints like Tukaram should not be taken in a literal sense. . . .

The moral is that we must realize the idea which underlies the words of holy men. It is quite possible that they worshipped the formless even while they pictured God in a particular form. This is impossible for ordinary mortals like ourselves, and therefore we would be in a sorry plight if we did not penetrate a little deeper into the implications of their statements.

The Diary of Mahadev Desai, vol. I (1953), pp. 168-69

Mortal man can only imagine the unmanifest, the impersonal, and as his language fails him he often negatively describes it as, *"Neti, neti."* [Not that, not that.] And so even iconoclasts are at bottom no better than idol-worshippers. To worship a book, to go to a church, or to pray with one's face in a particular direction — all these are forms of worshipping the formless in an image or idol. And yet both the idol-breaker and the idol-worshipper cannot lose sight of the fact that there is something which is beyond all form, unthinkable, formless, impersonal, changeless. The highest goal of the devotee is to become one with the object of his devotion. The *bhakta* extinguishes himself and merges into, becomes, Bhagavan. This state can best be reached by devoting oneself to some form, and so it is said that the short cut to the unmanifest is really the longest and the most difficult.

The Gita According to Gandhi (1956), pp. 308-09

63. Idol Worship

I do not disbelieve in idol worship. An idol does not excite any feeling of veneration in me. But I think that idol worship is part of human nature. We hanker after symbolism. Why should one be more composed in a church than elsewhere? Images are an aid to worship. . . . I do not consider idol worship a sin.

Young India, October 6, 1921

It is being more and more demonstrated that it is the worship of God, be it in the crudest manner possible, which distinguishes man from the brute. It is the possession of that additional quality which gives him such enormous hold upon God's creation. It is wholly irrelevant to show that millions of educated people never enter a church, mosque or temple. Such entry is neither natural nor indispensable for the worship of God. Those even who bow their heads before stocks and stones, who believe in incantations or ghosts, acknowledge a power above and beyond them. It is true that this form of worship is savage, very crude; nevertheless, it is worship of God.

Gold is still gold though in its crudest state. It merely awaits refinement to be treated as gold even by the ignorant. No amount of refinement will turn iron ore into gold. Refined worship is doubtless due to the effort of man. Crude worship is as old as Adam, and as natural to him as eating and drinking, if not more natural. A man may live without eating for days on end; he does not live without worship for a single minute. He may not acknowledge the fact, as many an ignorant man may not acknowledge the possession of lungs or the fact of the circulation of blood.

Young India, July 8, 1926

64. Idolatry

(By Mahadev Desai)
Gandhiji: As for idol worship, you cannot do without it in some form or other. Why does a Musalman give his life for defending a mosque which he calls a house of God? And why does a Christian go to a church, and when he is required to take an oath he swears by the Bible? Not that I see any objection to it. . . . And what do the Roman Catholics do when they kneel before Virgin Mary and before saints — quite imaginary figures in stone or

painted on canvas or glass?

Catholic Father: But I keep my mother's photo and kiss it in veneration of her. But I do not worship it, nor do I worship saints. When I worship God, I acknowledge him as creator and greater than any human being.

G: Even so, it is not the stone we worship, but it is God we worship in images of stone or metal, however crude they may be.

C: But villagers worship stones as God.

G: No. I tell you they do not worship anything that is less than God. When you kneel before Virgin Mary and ask for her intercession, what do you do? You ask to establish contact with God through her. Even so a Hindu seeks to establish contact with God through a stone image. I can understand your asking for the Virgin's intercession. Why are Musalmans filled with awe and exultation when they enter a mosque? Why is not the whole universe a mosque? And what about the magnificent canopy of heaven that spreads over you? Is it any less than a mosque? But I understand and sympathize with the Muslims. It is their way of approach to God. The Hindus have their own way of approach to the same eternal being. Our media of approach are different, but that does not make [our Gods] different.

C: But the Catholics believe that God revealed to them the true way.

G: But why do you say that the will of God is expressed only in one book called the Bible and not in others? Why do you circumscribe the ponver of God?

C: But Jesus proved that he had received the word of God through miracles.

G: But that is Mohammed's claim too. If you accept Christian testimony you must accept Muslim testimony and Hindu testimony too.

C: But Mohammed said he could not do miracles.

G: No. He did not want to prove the existence of God by miracles. But he claimed to receive messages from God.

When one comes to think of it, how simple and naive is man's fanaticism! "The attempt to make the one religion which is their own dominate all time and space comes naturally to men addicted to sectarianism," said Gurudeva Rabindranath Tagore at the Parliament of Religions in Calcutta. "This makes it offensive to them to be told that God is generous in his distribution of love, and his means of communication with men have not been restricted to a blind lane abruptly stopping at one narrow point of history. If humanity ever happens to be overwhelmed with the universal flood of a bigoted exclusiveness, then God will have to make provision for another Noah's ark to save his creatures from the catastrophe of spiritual desolation."
Harijan, March 13, 1937

65. Worship in Temples

Q: You seem to advocate the starting of temples for [untouchables] as a step in the direction of their amelioration. Is it not a fact that the Hindu mind, confined for generations past within things like the "temple" has generally lost the power of any larger vision of God? When you seek to remove untouchability, when you seek to raise the untouchables and accord them a place of freedom and dignity in society, need you do so by encouraging them to copy the present-day caste Hindus even in the matter of the latter's vices, sins and superstitions?

In the course of ameliorating the untouchables may we not also reform the Hindu community as a whole, so far at least as worship of temple gods is concerned? In the course of freeing the depressed classes from their present social disabilities, may we not seek also to free their mind and thought, and thus let social reforms bring into being a broader religious and intellectual outlook?

A: I do not regard the existence of temples as a sin or

superstition. Some form of common worship, and a common place of worship appear to be a human necessity. Whether the temples should contain images or not is a matter of temperament and taste. I do not regard a Hindu or a Roman Catholic place of worship containing images as necessarily bad or superstitious and a mosque or a Protestant place of worship being good or free of superstition merely because of their exclusion of images. A symbol such as a cross or a book may easily become idolatrous, and therefore superstitious. And the worship of the image of child Krishna or Virgin Mary may become ennobling and free of all superstition. It depends upon the attitude of the heart of the worshipper.

Young India, November 5, 1925

66. Are Temples Necessary?

An American correspondent writes:

"My reading of the history of religion is that every great religious advance has been away from organized and formal religion. The great religious truths which the prophets of religion have apprehended and proclaimed have always been lost when their disciples have tried to localize them in priestcraft and temples. Truth is too universal to be confined and made sectarian. Therefore, I consider temples, mosques and churches to be a prostitution of religion. In every nation we have witnessed the degradation of truth and righteousness in the temples; and, in my opinion, in the very conception of organized religion this is certain to follow as a natural consequence. When religion is made a monopoly by the priesthood and temples become vested interests, the great mass of mankind becomes isolated from truth until some new prophets arise who break the bonds of orthodoxy and release the spirits of men from dependence upon the priests and temples.

"Buddha and Jesus, Chaitanya and Kabir realized and taught truth, which is universal in its character and helpful to all men everywhere, but the 'isms which bear their names are exclusive and divisive and, therefore, harmful to those who accept the priestly interpretations of these teachings. Religion loses its human character and deserves its reputation of being called an opiate.

"Therefore, I can see no advantage in gaining permission for the *harijan* [lit. child of god; the poor] to enter the temples. I know that justice demands that they shall have the liberty even to do wrong. But if they are to learn the lessons of self-respect which will enable them to take an equal place with caste people in the development of the future of our civilization, I think they must learn an independence of all priests and temples. They must attain a self-realization, which is dependent upon inner rather than outer forces.

"In the process there is likely to be some extravagance of defiance and bitterness before they actually find themselves. When you spoke in Europe that you formerly considered that God is truth but now you realized that truth is God, you struck a responsive chord in the hearts of all of us, whatever our traditions may have been. But when you become a defender of the faith of temple Hinduism, even though it be a purified type, we feel that you have lost your universal appeal, an appeal which I consider you to have made as a Hindu, but as one of that large body of spiritual-minded Hindus who do not look to the temples for the spiritual sustenance of their lives. I do not believe that such men are outside the best traditions of Hinduism but are rather in the line of the creators of the religious spirit which has made the spirituality of India her greatest contribution to humanity.

"Nor do I believe that this higher Hinduism is too high for the *harijans*, whose spiritual intuitions have never been dulled by our modern type of education. Buddha, Chaitanya and Kabir all made a large appeal to this class, and the teachings of Jesus were most appreciated, not by the high and mighty, but by publicans and fishermen who were outside the pale of respectable society. If you were to challenge the untouchables to keep as before outside the temples and refuse to accept an inferior status in society by defying the caste leaders, and encourage them to develop their inner resources, I think you would have the support of just as large a community of Hindus as you have in your present programme"

This considered opinion representing a large body of people throughout the world deserves respectful consideration. Such an opinion, however, does not appear before me for the first time. I have had the privilege and opportunity of discussing this subject with many friends in the light it is presented. I can appreciate much of the argument, but I venture to think that it is inconclusive, because it has omitted material facts. Some priests are bad. Temples, churches and mosques very often show corruption, more often deterioration. Nevertheless, it would be impossible to prove that all priests are bad or have been bad and that all churches, temples and mosques are hot-beds of corruption and superstition. Nor does the argument take note of this fundamental fact — that no faith has done without a habitation. And I go further that in the very nature of things it cannot exist, so long as man remains as he is constituted. His very body has been rightly called the temple of the Holy Ghost, though innumerable such temples belie the fact and are hot-beds of corruption used for dissoluteness. And I presume that it will be accepted as a conclusive answer to a sweeping suggestion that all bodies should be destroyed for the corruption of many, if it can be shown, as it can be, that there are some bodies which are proper temples of the Holy Ghost.

The cause for the corruption of many bodies will have to be sought elsewhere. Temples of stone and mortar are nothing else than a natural extension of these human temples and though they were in their conception undoubtedly habitations of God like human temples, they have been subject to the same law of decay as the latter.

I know of no religion or sect that has done or is doing without its house of God, variously described as a temple, mosque, church, synagogue or agiari. Nor is it certain that any of the great reformers including Jesus destroyed or discarded temples altogether. All of them sought to banish corruption from temples as well as from society. Some of them, if not all, appear to have preached from temples. I have ceased to visit temples for years, but I do not regard myself on that account as a better person than before. My mother never missed going to the temple, when she was in a fit state to go there. Probably her faith was far greater than mine, though I do not visit temples. There are millions whose faith is sustained through these temples, churches and mosques. They are not all blind followers of a superstition, nor are they fanatics. . . .

My advocacy of temple entry I hold to be perfectly consistent with the declaration which I often made in Europe that truth is God. It is that belief which makes it possible, at the risk of losing friendships, popularity and prestige, to advocate temple entry for *harijans*. The truth that I know or I feel I know demands that advocacy from me. Hinduism loses its right to make a universal appeal if it closes its temples to the *harijans*.

That temples and temple worship are in need of radical reform must be admitted. But all reform without temple entry will be to tamper with the disease. I am aware that the American friend's objection is not based upon the corruption or impurity of the temples. His objection is much more radical. He does not believe in them at all. I have endeavoured to show that his position is untenable in the light of facts which can be verified from everyday experience. To reject the necessity of temples is to reject the necessity of God, religion and earthly existence.

Harijan, March 11, 1933

67. Are Places of Worship a Superstition?

A correspondent writes thus passionately:

"I am afraid, there is a little fly in the ointment of your splendid defense [see 19. No Faith in Prayer] of the practice of divine prayer, especially congregational prayer. At the end of the article, referring to churches, temples and mosques you say these places of worship are not a mere idle superstition to be swept away at the first opportunity. They have survived all attacks up to now and are likely to persist to the end of time.

"On reading this I asked myself, attacks by whom? Surely those attacks were not made by atheists or scoffers or humbugs to anything like the extent to which the opposing sects of God-believers are known to have attacked the places of worship of one another. In fact, most, if not all, of the attacks you speak of were perpetrated by 'godly' zealots in the name and for the glory of each one's own God. It would be insulting your knowledge of world history to cite instances.

"Secondly, I asked myself: Is it true — is it strictly correct — to say, that these places of worship have survived all attacks? Again the answer is, surely not. Witness the site at Kashi (or Banaras) where had stood the temple of Vishwanath for long centuries, since even before Lord Buddha's time — but where now stands dominating the 'Holy City' — a mosque built out of the ruins of the desecrated old temple by orders of no less a man than the 'Living Saint', the 'Ascetic King', the 'Puritan Emperor' — Aurangazeb.

"Again, it is not the 'unbelieving' British, but the terrible believer, Ibn Saud, and his Wahabi hosts, that are responsible for the recent demolition and desecration of many places of worship in the Muslim's 'Holy Land', over which Musalman Indians are just now so loudly lamenting, and which the Nizam of Hyderabad — alone of all Muslim rulers in the world — has vainly tried to restore with his money.

"Do these facts mean nothing to you, Mahatmaji?"

These facts do mean a great deal to me. They show undoubtedly man's barbarity. But they chasten me. They warn me against becoming intolerant. And they make me tolerant even towards the intolerant. They show man's utter insignificance and thus drive him to pray, if he will not be led to it. For does not history record instances of humbled pride bending the knee before the almighty, washing his feet with tears of blood and asking to be reduced to dust under his heels? Verily "the letter killeth, the spirit giveth life."

The writer, who is one of the most regular and painstaking readers of *Young India*, should know by this time that places of worship to me are not merely brick and mortar. They are but a shadow of the reality. Against every church and every mosque and every temple destroyed, hundreds have risen in their places. It is wholly irrelevant to the argument about the necessity of prayer that the so-called believers have belied their belief and that many places renowned for their sacred character have been razed to the ground. I hold it to be enough, and it is enough for my argument, if I can prove that there have been men in the world, and there are men today in existence, for whom prayer is positively the bread of life.

I recommend to the correspondent the practice of going unobserved to mosques, temples and churches, without any preconceived ideas, and he will discover as I have discovered that there is something in them which appeals to the heart and which transforms those who go there, not for show, not out of shame or fear, but out of simple devotion. It defies analysis. Nevertheless the fact stands that pure-minded people going to the present places of pilgrimage which have become hot-beds of error, superstition, and even immorality, return from them purer for the act of worship. Hence the significant assurance in the Bhagavadgita: "I make return according to the spirit in which men worship me."

What the correspondent has written undoubtedly shows our present limitations, which we must try as early as possible to get rid of. It is a plea for purification of religions, broadening of the outlook. That much-needed reform is surely coming. There is a better world consciousness, and may I say that even the reform we all hanker after needs intense prayer in order to achieve deeper purification of self? For without deeper purification of mankind in general, mutual toleration and mutual goodwill are not possible.

Young India, April 11, 1926

68. Why No Temple in the Ashram?

You did well in writing to me regarding the temple. If you have still something more to say, write to me. I surely don't insist that my view in this matter should prevail. However, my views on this subject are fixed. I have said regarding myself that I am both an image worshipper and an image breaker. The God conceived by a human being is bound to be a form, though the image may be only in the mind. In that sense, I am an image worshipper. But I have never been willing to worship any form or image as God. Towards a form or image, I always feel *neti, neti*. [Not this, not this.] Hence I regard myself as image breaker. This being my attitude, I have always felt that we should not have any temple in the ashram. And it was for this reason that we decided to have no building even for prayers. We sit in the open, with the sky above as the roof and the horizons on the four sides as the walls. If we wish to maintain an attitude of equality towards all religions, this is how we should live. These days, I am trying to read a little from the Vedas and other sacred books. I see this same thing in them all. There is no mention of image worship anywhere. But Hinduism has a place for it. We should not, therefore, oppose it. However, image worship is not obligatory. It is voluntary. I feel, therefore, that it would be better if, as an institution, we kept away from image worship.

Collected Works — LI (1972), p, 10

69. Nature's Temple of Worship

Here in Ceylon where I am writing for *Young India* amid surroundings where nature has bountifully poured her richest treasures, I recall a letter written by a poetically-inclined friend from similar scenes. I share with the reader a paragraph:

"A lovely morning! Cool, cloudy, with a drowsy sun whose rays are soft as velvet. It is a strangely quiet morning — there is a hush upon it, as of prayer. And the mists are like incense, and the trees worshippers in a trance, and the birds and insects pilgrims come to chant *bhajans*. Oh! how I wish one could learn true abandonment from nature! We seem to have forgotten our birthright to worship where and when and how we please. We build temples and mosques and churches to keep our worship safe from prying eyes and away from outside influences, but we forget that walls have eyes and ears, and the roofs might be swarming with ghosts — who knows!

"Good Gracious, I shall find myself preaching next! How foolish, on a lovely morning like this? A little child in the garden adjoining is singing as unconsciously and joyously as a bird. I feel inclined to go and take the dust of its little feet. And since I cannot pour out my heart in sound as simply as that little one, my only refuge is in silence!"

Churches, mosques and temples, which cover so much hypocrisy and humbug and shut the poorest out of them, seem but a mockery of God and his worship, when one sees the eternally-renewed temple of worship under the vast blue canopy inviting every one of us to real worship, instead of abusing his name by quarrelling in the name of religion.

Young India, December 8, 1927

70. Tree Worship

A correspondent writes:

"It is a common enough sight in this country to see men and women offering worship to stocks and stones and trees, but I was surprised to find that even educated women belonging to the families of enthusiastic social workers were not above this practice. Some of these sisters and friends defend the practice by saying that since it is founded on pure reverence for the divine in nature and no false beliefs, it cannot be classed as superstition, and they cite the names of Satyavan and Savitri whose memory, they say, they commemorate in that way. The argument does not convince me. May I request you to throw some light on the matter?"

I like this question. It raises the old, old question of image worship. I am both a supporter and opponent of image worship. When image worship degenerates into idolatry and becomes encrusted with false beliefs and doctrines, it becomes a necessity to combat it as a gross social evil. On the other hand image worship in the sense of investing one's ideal with a concrete shape is inherent in man's nature, and even valuable as an aid to devotion.

Thus we worship an image when we offer homage to a book which we regard as holy or sacred. We worship an image when we visit a temple or a mosque with a feeling of sanctity or reverence. Nor do I see any harm in all this. On the contrary endowed as man is with a finite, limited understanding, he can hardly do otherwise.

Even so far from seeing anything inherently evil or harmful in tree worship, I find in it a thing instinct with a deep pathos and poetic beauty. It symbolizes true reverence for the entire vegetable kingdom, which with its endless panorama of beautiful shapes and forms, declares to us as it were with a million tongues the greatness and glory of God. Without vegetation our planet would not be able to support life even for a moment. In such a country especially, therefore, in which there is a scarcity of trees, tree worship assumes a profound economic significance.

I, therefore, see no necessity for leading a crusade against tree worship. It is true that the poor, simple-minded women who offer worship to trees have no reasoned understanding of the implications of their act. Possibly they would not be able to give any explanation as to why they perform it. They act in the purity and utter simplicity of their faith. Such faith is not a thing to be despised; it is a great and powerful force that we should treasure.

Far different, however, is the case of vows and prayers which votaries offer before trees. The offering of vows and prayers for selfish ends, whether offered in churches, mosques, temples or before trees and shrines, is a thing not to be encouraged. Making of selfish requests or offering of vows is not related to image-worship as effect and cause. A personal, selfish prayer is bad whether made before an image or an unseen God.

Let no one, however, from this understand me to mean that I advocate tree worship in general. I do not defend tree worship because I consider it to be a necessary aid to devotion, but only because I recognize that God manifests himself in innumerable forms in this universe, and every such manifestation commands my spontaneous reverence.

Young India, September 16, 1929

71. Atmosphere for Prayers

My prayers here [first-class on a ship] lack the depth, the serenity and concentration they had when I was in gaol. I am not writing all this in a frivolous mood, but after deep reflection. I think of these things everyday. . . .

I have realized that those who wish to serve God cannot afford to pamper themselves or to run after luxury. Prayers do not come easily in an atmosphere of luxuries. Even if we do not ourselves share the luxuries, we cannot escape their natural influence. The energy that we spend in resisting that influence is at the cost of our devotional efforts.

Collected Works — IX (1963), pp. 276-77

72. The Place of Prayer in Ashram Life

If insistence on truth constitutes the root of the ashram, prayer is the principal feeder of that root. The social (as distinguished from the individual) activities of the ashram commence every day with the congregational morning worship at 4:15 to 4:45 A.M. and close with the evening prayer at 7 to 7.30 P.M. Ever since the ashram was founded, not a single day has passed to my knowledge without this worship. I know of several occasions when owing to the rains only one responsible person was present on the prayer ground. All inmates are expected to attend the worship except in the case of illness or similar compelling reason for absence. This expectation has been fairly well fulfilled at the evening prayer, but not in the morning.

The time for morning worship was as a matter of experiment fixed at 4, 5, 6 and 7 A.M., one after another. But on account of my persistently strong attitude on the subject, it has been fixed at last at 4:20 A.M. With the first bell at 4 everyone rises from bed and after a wash reaches the prayer ground by 4:20.

I believe that in a country like India the sooner a man rises from bed the better. Indeed millions must necessarily rise early. If the peasant is a late riser, his crops will suffer damage. Cattle are attended to and cows are milked early in the morning. Such being the case, seekers of saving truth, servants of the people or monks may well be up at 2 or 3; it would be surprising if they are not. In all countries of the world devotees of God and tillers of the soil rise early. Devotees take the name of God and peasants work in their fields serving the world as well as themselves. To my mind both are worshippers. Devotees are deliberately such while cultivators by their industry worship God unawares, as it helps to sustain the world. If instead of working in the fields, they took to meditation, they would be failing in their duty and involving themselves and the world in ruin.

We may or may not look upon the cultivator as a devotee, but where peasants, laborers and other people have willy-nilly to rise early, how can a worshipper of truth or servant of the people be a late riser? Again in the ashram we are trying to coordinate work and worship. Therefore I am definitely of opinion that all able-bodied people in the ashram must rise early even at the cost of inconvenience. Four A.M. is not early but the latest time when we must be up and doing.

Then again we had to take a decision on certain questions. Where should the prayers be offered? Should we erect a temple or meet in the open air? Then again, should we raise a platform or sit in the sands or the dust? Should there be any images? At last we decided to sit on the sands under the canopy of the sky and not to install any image. Poverty is an ashram observance. The ashram exists in order to serve the starving millions. The poor have a place in it no less than others. It receives with open arms all who are willing to keep the rules, In such an institution the house of worship cannot be built with bricks and mortar, the sky must suffice for roof and the quarters for walls and pillars. A platform was planned but discarded later on, as its size would depend upon the indeterminate number of worshippers. And a big one would cost a large sum of money. Experience has shown the soundness of the decision not to build a house or even a platform. People from outside also attend the ashram prayers, so that at times the multitude present cannot be accommodated on the biggest of platforms.

Again as the ashram prayers are being increasingly imitated

elsewhere, the sky-roofed temple has proved its utility. Morning and evening prayers are held wherever I go. Then there is such large attendance, especially in the evening, that prayers are possible only on open grounds. And if I had been in the habit of worshipping in a prayer hall only, I might perhaps never have thought of public prayers during my tours.

Then again all religions are accorded equal respect in the ashram. Followers of all faiths are welcome there; they may or may not believe in the worship of images. No image is kept at the congregational worship of the ashram in order to avoid hurting anybody's feelings. But if an ashramite wishes to keep an image in his room, he is free to do so

* * *

At the morning prayer we first recite the shlokas [verses] printed in *Ashram Bhajanavali* [hymnal], and then sing one *bhajan* [hymn] followed by *Ramdhun* [repetition of Ramanama] and *Gitapath* [recitation of the Gita]. In the evening we have recitation of the last nineteen verses of the second chapter of the Gita, one *bhajan* and *Ramdhun*, and then read some portion of a sacred book.

The shlokas were selected by Shri Kaka Kalelkar who has been in the ashram since its foundation. Shri Maganlal Gandhi met him in Santiniketan [the ashram of poet Rabindranath Tagore] when he and the children of the Phoenix Settlement went there from South Africa while I was still in England. Dinabandhu Andrews and the late Mr. Pearson were then in Santiniketan. I had advised Maganlal to stay at some place selected by Andrews. And Andrews selected Santiniketan for the party. Kaka was a teacher there and came into close contact with Maganlal. Maganlal had been feeling the want of a Sanskrit teacher which was supplied by Kaka. Chintamani Shastri assisted him in the work. Kaka taught the children how to recite the verses repeated in prayer. Some of these verses were omitted in the ashram prayer in order to save time. Such is the history of the verses recited at the morning prayer all these days.

The recitation of these verses has often been objected to on the ground of saving time or because it appeared to some people that they could not well be recited by a worshipper of truth or by a non-Hindu. There is no doubt that these verses are recited only in Hindu society, but I cannot see why a non-Hindu may not join in or be present at the recitation. Muslim and Christian friends who have heard the verses have not raised any objection. Indeed they need not cause annoyance to anyone who respects other faiths as much as he respects his own. They do not contain any reflection on other people. Hindus being in an overwhelming majority in the ashram, the verses must be selected from the sacred books of the Hindus. Not that nothing is sung or recited from non-Hindu scriptures. Indeed there were occasions on which Imam Saheb recited verses from the Koran. Muslim and Christian hymns are often sung.

But the verses were strongly attacked from the standpoint of truth. An ashramite modestly but firmly argued that the worship of Sarasvati, Ganesh and the like was violence done to truth; for no such divinities really existed as Sarasvati seated on a lotus with a *vina* [kind of musical instrument] in her hands, or as Ganesh with a big belly and an elephant's trunk. To this argument I replied as follows:

"I claim to be a votary of truth, and yet I do not mind reciting these verses or teaching them to the children. If we condemn some shlokas on the strength of this argument, it would be tantamount to an attack on the very basis of Hinduism. Not that we may not condemn anything in Hinduism which is fit for condemnation, no matter how ancient it is. But I do not believe that this is a weak or vulnerable point of Hinduism. On the other hand I hold that it is perhaps characteristic of our faith. Sarasvati and Ganesh are not independent entities. They are all descriptive names of one God. Devoted poets have given a local habitation and a name to his countless attributes. They have done nothing wrong. Such verses deceive neither the worshippers nor others. When a human being praises God he imagines him to be such as he thinks fit. The God of his imagination is there for him. Even when we pray to a God devoid of form and attributes we do in fact endow him with attributes. And attributes too are form. Fundamentally God is indescribable in words. We mortals must of necessity depend upon the imagination which makes and sometimes mars us too. The qualities we attribute to God with the purest of motives are true for us but fundamentally false, because all attempts at describing him must be unsuccessful.

"I am intellectually conscious of this and still I cannot help dwelling upon the attributes of God. My intellect can exercise no influence over my heart. I am prepared to admit that my heart in its weakness hankers after a God with attributes. The shlokas which I have been reciting every day for the last fifteen years give me peace and hold good for me. In them I find beauty as well as poetry. Learned men tell many stories about Sarasvati, Ganesh and the like, which have their own use. I do not know their deeper meaning, as I have not gone into it, finding it unnecessary for me. It may be that my ignorance is my salvation. I did not see that I needed to go deep into this as a part of my quest of truth. It is enough that I know my God, and although I have still to realize His living presence, I am on the right path to my destination."

I could hardly expect that the objectors should be satisfied with this reply. An ad hoc committee examined the whole question fully and finally recommended that the shlokas should remain as they were, for every possible selection would be viewed with disfavor by someone or other.

✻   ✻   ✻

A hymn was sung after the shlokas. Indeed singing hymns was the only item of the prayers in South Africa. The shlokas were added in India. Maganlal Gandhi was our leader in song. But we felt that the arrangement was unsatisfactory. We should have an expert singer for the purpose, and that singer should be one who would observe the ashram rules. One such was found in Narayan Moreshwar Khare, a pupil of Pandit Vishnu Digambar, whom the master kindly sent to the ashram. Pandit Khare gave us full satisfaction and is now a full member of the ashram. He made hymn singing interesting, and the *Ashram Bhajanavali* [hymnal] which is now read by thousands was in the main compiled by him. He introduced *Ramdhun*, the third item of our prayers.

The fourth item is recitation of verses from the Gita. The Gita has for years been an authoritative guide to belief and conduct for the Satyagraha Ashram. It has provided us with a test with which to determine the correctness or otherwise of ideas and courses of conduct in question. Therefore we wished that all ashramites should understand the meaning of the Gita and if possible commit it to memory. If this last was not possible, we wished that they should at least read the original Sanskrit with correct pronunciation. With this end in view we began to recite part of the Gita every day. We would recite a few verses every day and continue the recitation until we had learnt them by heart.

The recitation is now so arranged that the whole of the Gita is finished in fourteen days, and everybody knows what verses will be recited on any particular day. The first chapter is recited on every alternate Friday, and we shall come to it on Friday next (June 10, 1932). The seventh and eighth, the twelfth and thirteenth, the fourteenth and fifteenth, and the sixteenth and seventeenth chapters are recited on the same day in order to finish eighteen chapters in fourteen days.

At the evening prayer we recite the last nineteen verses of the second chapter of the Gita as well as sing a hymn and repeat Ramanama. These verses describe the characteristics of the *sthitaprajna* [the man of stable understanding], which a satyagrahi too must acquire, and are recited in order that he may constantly bear them in mind.

Repeating the same thing at prayer from day to day is objected to on the ground that it thus becomes mechanical and tends to be ineffective. It is true that the prayer becomes mechanical. We ourselves are machines, and if we believe God to be our mover, we must behave like machines in his hands. If the sun and other heavenly bodies did not work like machines, the universe would come to a standstill. But in behaving like machines, we must not behave like inert matter. We are intelligent beings and must observe rules as such.

The point is not whether the contents of the prayer are always the same or differ from day to day. Even if they are full of variety, it is possible that they will become ineffective. The *Gayatri* verse among Hindus, the confession of faith, *kalma*, among Mussalmans, the typical Christian prayer in the Sermon on the Mount, have been recited by millions for centuries every day; and yet their power has not diminished but is ever on the increase.

It all depends upon the spirit behind the recitation. If an unbeliever or a parrot repeats these potent words, they will fall quite flat. On the other hand when a believer utters them always, their influence grows from day to day. Our staple food is the same. The wheat eater will take other things besides wheat, and these additional things may differ from time to time, but the wheat bread will always be there on the dining table. It is the eater's staff of life, and he will never weary of it. If he conceives a dislike for it, that is a sign of the approaching dissolution of his body.

The same is the case with prayer. Its principal contents must be always the same. If the soul hungers after them, she will not quarrel with the monotony of the prayer but will derive nourishment from it. She will have a sense of deprivation on the day that it has not been possible to offer prayer. She will be more downcast than one who observes a physical fast. Giving up food may now and then be beneficial for the body; indigestion of prayer for the soul is something never heard of.

The fact is that many of us offer prayer without our soul being hungry for it. It is a fashion to believe that there is a soul; so we believe that she exists. Such is the sorry plight of many among us. Some are intellectually convinced that there is a soul, but they have not grasped that truth with the heart; therefore they do not feel the need for prayer. Many offer prayer because they live in society and think they must participate in its activities. No wonder they hanker after variety. As a matter of fact however they do not attend prayer. They want to enjoy the music or are merely curious or wish to listen to the sermon. They are not there to be one with God.

*   *   *

Prarthana [Gujarati word for prayer] literally means to ask for something, that is, to ask God for something in a spirit of humility. Here it is not used in that sense, but in the sense of praising or worshipping God, meditation and self-purification.

But who is God? God is not some person outside ourselves or away from the universe. He pervades everything, and is omniscient as well as omnipotent. He does not need any praise or petitions. Being immanent in all beings, he hears everything and reads our innermost thoughts. He abides in our hearts and is nearer to us than the nails are to the fingers. What is the use of telling him anything?

It is in view of this difficulty that *prarthana* is further paraphrased as self-purification. When we speak out aloud at prayer time, our speech is addressed not to God but to ourselves, and is intended to shake off our torpor. Some of us are intellectually aware of God, while others are afflicted by doubt. None has seen him face to face. We desire to recognize and realize him, to become one with him, and seek to gratify that desire through prayer.

This God whom we seek to realize is truth. Or to put it in another way truth is God. This truth is not merely the truth we are expected to speak. It is that which alone is, which constitutes the stuff of which all things are made, which subsists by virtue of its own power, which is not supported by anything else but supports everything that exists. Truth alone is eternal, everything else is momentary. It need not assume shape or form. It is pure intelligence as well as pure bliss. We call It Ishvara because everything is regulated by its will. It and the law it promulgates are one. Therefore it is not a blind law. It governs the entire universe. To propitiate this truth is *prarthana*, which in effect means an earnest desire to be filled with the spirit of truth. This desire should be present all the twenty-four hours. But our souls are too dull to have this awareness day and night. Therefore we offer prayers for a short time in the hope that a time will come when all our conduct will be one continuously sustained prayer.

Such is the ideal of prayer for the ashram, which at present is far, far away from it. The detailed program outlined above is something external, but the idea is to make our very hearts prayerful. If the ashram prayers are not still attractive, if even the inmates of the ashram attend them under compulsion of a sort, it only means that none of us is still a man of prayer in the real sense of the term.

In heartfelt prayer the worshipper's attention is concentrated on the object of worship so much so that he is not conscious of anything else besides. The worshipper has well been compared to a lover. The lover forgets the whole world and even himself in the presence of the beloved. The identification of the worshipper with God should be closer still. It comes only after much striving, self-suffering, *tapas* [self-control], and self-discipline. In a place which such a worshipper sanctifies by his presence, no inducements need be offered to people for attending prayers, as they are drawn to the house of prayer by the force of his devotion.

We have dealt so far with congregational prayer, but great stress is also laid in the ashram on individual and solitary prayer. One who never prays by himself may attend congregational prayers but will not derive much advantage from them. They are absolutely necessary for a congregation, but as a congregation is made up of individuals, they are fruitless without individual prayers. Every member of the ashram is therefore reminded now and then that he should of his own accord give himself up to self-introspection at all times of the day. No watch can be kept that he does this, and no account can be maintained of such silent prayer. I cannot say how far it prevails in the ashram, but I believe that some are making effort in that direction.

Ashram Observances in Action (1959), Chapter Two

73. The Ashram Prayer

The ashram prayer has become very popular. Its development has been spontaneous. The *Ashram Bhajanavali* [hymn book] has gone into several editions and is increasingly in demand. The birth and growth of this prayer has not been artificial. There is a history attached to almost every shloka and every selected *bhajan*. The *Bhajanavali* contains, among others, *bhajans* from Muslim *sufis* and *fakirs*, from Guru Nanak, and from the Christian hymnary. Every religion seems to have found a natural setting in the prayer book.

Chinese, Burmese, Jews, Ceylonese, Muslims, Parsis, Europeans and Americans have all lived in the ashram from time to time. In the same way two Japanese sadhus [monks] came to me in Maganwadi in 1935. One of them was with me till the other day when war broke out with Japan. He was an ideal inmate of our home in Sevagram. He took part in every activity with zest. I never heard of his quarrelling with anyone. He was a silent worker. He learnt as much Hindi as he could. He was a strict observer of his vows. Every morning and evening he could be seen going round with his drum and heard chanting his mantra. The evening worship always commenced with his mantra, "I bow to the Buddha, the giver of true religion." I shall never forget the quickness, the orderliness and utter detachment with which he prepared himself the day the police came without notice to take him away from the ashram.

He took leave of me after reciting his favourite mantra and left his drum with me. "You are leaving us, but your mantra will remain an integral part of our ashram prayer," were the words that came spontaneously to my lips. Since then, in spite of his absence, our morning and evening worship has commenced with the mantra. For me it is a constant reminder of Sadhu Keshav's purity and single-eyed devotion. Indeed its efficacy lies in that sacred memory.

While Sadhu Keshav was still with us, Bibi Raihana Tyabji also came to stay at Sevagram for a few days. I knew her to be a devout Muslim but was not aware, before the death of her illustrious father, of how well-versed she was in Koran Sharif. When that jewel of Gujarat, Tyabji Saheb, expired, no sound of weeping broke the awful silence in his room. The latter echoed with Bibi Raihana's sonorous recitation of verses from the Koran. Such as Abbas Tyabji Saheb cannot die. He is ever alive in the example of national service which he has left behind. Bibi Raihana is an accomplished singer with an ample repertory of *bhajans* of all kinds. She used to sing daily as well as recite beautiful verses from the Koran. I asked her to teach some verses to any of the inmates who could learn them, and she gladly did so. Like so many who come here she had become one of us. Raihana went away when her visit was over, but she has left a fragrant reminder of herself. The well-known *Al Fateha* has been included in the ashram worship. The following is a translation of it:

I take refuge in Allah
from Satan the accursed.

Say he is God, the one and only God,
the eternal, absolute.
He begetteth not nor is he begotten,
And there is none like unto him.

Praise be to God,
The cherisher and sustainer of the worlds,
most gracious, most merciful,
master of the day of judgment.
Thee do we worship
And thine aid we seek.
Show us the straight way,
The way of those on whom
Thou hast bestowed thy grace,
Those whose portion is not wrath
And who go not astray.

I am writing this note in reply to an ardent Hindu friend who thus gently reproached me: "You have now given the Kalma a place in the ashram. What further remains to be done to kill your Hinduism?"

I am confident that my Hinduism and that of the other ashram Hindus has grown thereby. There should be in us an equal reverence for all religions. Badshah Khan, whenever he comes, joins in the worship here with delight. He loves the tune to which the Ramayana is sung, and he listens intently to the Gita. His faith in Islam has not lessened thereby. Then why may I not listen to the Koran with equal reverence and adoration in my heart?

Vinoba and Pyarelal studied Arabic and leamt the Koran in jail. Their Hinduism has been enriched by this study. I believe that Hindu-Muslim unity will come only through such spontaneous mingling of hearts and no other. Rama is not known by only a thousand names. His names are innumerable and he is the same whether we call him Allah, Khuda, Rahim, Razzak, the Breadgiver, or any name that comes from the heart.

Harijan, February 15, 1942

During the three days I passed in Shrinagar, though I had prayers in the compound of Lala Kishorilal's bungalow where I was accommodated, I made no speeches. I had so declared before leaving Delhi. But some of the audience sent me questions:

"I attended your prayer meeting last evening in which you recited two prayers of the other communities. May I know what is your idea in doing so and what you mean by a religion?"

As I have observed before now, the selection from the Koran was introduced some years ago on the suggestion of Raihana Tyabji who was then living in the Sevagram Ashram and the one from the Parsi prayers at the instance of Dr. Gilder who recited the Parsi prayer on the break of my fast in the Aga Khan Palace during our detention. I am of opinion that the addition enriched the prayer. It reached the hearts of a larger audience than before. It certainly showed Hinduism in its broad and tolerant aspect. The questioner ought also to have asked why the prayer commenced with the Buddhist prayer in Japanese. The selections of the stanzas of the prayer has a history behind it befitting the sacred character. The Buddhist prayer was the prayer with which the whole of Sevagram resounded in the early morning when a good Japanese monk was staying at the Sevagram Ashram and who by his silent and dignified conduct had endeared himself to the inmates of the ashram.

Harijan, August 17, 1947

74. About Prayer at the Ashhram

What you say about prayer at the ashram is largely true. It is still a formal thing, soulless; but I continue it in the hope of it becoming a soulful thing. Human nature is much the same whether in the East or in the West. It does not therefore surprise me that you have not found anything special about prayers in the East and probably the ashram prayer is a hotchpot of something Eastern and something Western. As I have no prejudice against taking anything good from the West or against giving up anything bad in the East, there is an unconscious blending of the two. For a congregational life a congregational prayer is a necessity and, therefore, form also is necessary. It need not be considered on that account to be hypocritical or harmful. If the leader at such congregational prayer meetings is a good man the general level of the meeting is also good. The spiritual effect of an honest, intelligent attendance at such congregational prayers is undoubtedly great.

Congregational prayer is not intended to supplant individual prayer, which, as you well put it, must be heartfelt and never formal. It is there you are in tune with the Infinite. Congregational prayer is an aid to being in tune with the Infinite. For man, who is a social being, cannot find God unless he discharges social obligations and the obligation of coming to a common prayer meeting is perhaps the supremest. It is a cleansing process for the whole congregation. But, like all human institutions, if one does not take care, such meetings do become formal and even hypocritical. One has to devise methods of avoiding the formality and hypocrisy. In all, especially in spiritual matters, it is the personal equation that counts in the end.

The Collected Works — XXXVI (1970), pp. 304-05

Prayer is the very foundation of the ashram. We should, therefore, clearly understand what it means. If it is not offered from the heart, it is no prayer at all. We rarely see anybody dozing while eating. Prayer is a million times more important than food. If anybody dozes at prayer time, his condition must be pitiable indeed. If we miss the prayer, we should feel deeply pained. We should not mind if we miss a meal, but we should never miss a prayer. Missing a meal is sometimes beneficial for health. Omitting prayer never is.

If any person dozes at the time of prayer, feels lazy or talks with his neighbours while the prayer is going on, does not fix his attention on it and lets his thoughts wander, he has as good as absented himself from it. His physical presence is mere show. He is, therefore, doubly guilty; he has absented himself from the prayer and has deceived the people. To deceive means to act untruthfully, and, therefore, to violate the vow of truth.

If, however, anybody feels sleepy or bored against his will, what should he do? But this can never happen. If we run straight from the bed to the prayer meeting, we are bound to feel sleepy. Before going to the meeting, we should rouse ourselves fully and brush our teeth, and resolve to remain awake and alert. In the meeting we should not sit close to one another, should sit erect like a walking-stick, breathe slowly and, if we can speak the words correctly, join in reciting the verses or singing the *bhajans* silently to ourselves if not loudly. If we cannot do even this, we may go on repeating Ramanama. If we still cannot control our body, we should keep standing. No one, whether a grown-up person or a child, should feel shame in doing so. Grown-up persons should occasionally keep standing, even if they do not feel sleepy, in order to create an atmosphere in which nobody would feel ashamed of standing.

Everyone should make an effort and understand as soon as possible the meaning of what is recited or sung for prayer. Even if a person does not know Sanskrit, he should learn the meaning of each verse and meditate over it.

Collected Works — L (1972), pp. 68-69

75. Time Taken Up By Prayers

We must not grudge it. Islam enjoins five prayers a day each of which would take at least fifteen minutes, and at which the same verses have to be repeated. Christian prayers contain one permanent item which also takes fifteen minutes each time. In churches belonging to the Catholics and to the established church in England, devotions take at least half an hour in the morning, at noon and again in the evening. This is not too much for the devotee. Finally, none of us has now the right to modify the order of the various items in our prayers. The subject has been thoroughly discussed already, and the discussion closed. We have to learn to appreciate our prayers and make them an instrument of the beatific vision. We must derive our daily spiritual nutrition from them. Let us not think of changes but pour our whole soul into them, such as they are.

The Diary of Mahadev Desai, vol. I (1953), p. 219

Prayers have often been attacked, but they have been kept up for sixteen years. How much time do they take? How much of the time can be saved? Anyone who accepts the necessity of prayers will not grudge the time given to them.

Collected Works — XLIX (1972), p. 406

76. From Manibehn's Notes
[Taken by Miss Manibehn Patel at Gandhi's morning prayer-meetings for women in the Ashram during 1926.]

If a laborer does all his work dedicating it to God, then he can attain self-realization. Self-realization means purity of self.

Strictly speaking, only those who do bodily labor achieve self-realization, because "God is the strength of the weak." By "weak" is not meant "weak in body," though for them too their strength is God — but we should take it to mean weak in means and equipment.

The laborer must cultivate humility. An exclusive development of the intellect may lead to the development of a diabolic kind of intelligence. By doing merely intellectual work, we develop satanic tendencies. It is for this that the Gita says that he who eats without doing labor eats stolen food.

Humility is inherent in each act of labor. And that is why it is *karmayoga*, or activity that leads to salvation. Doing physical work simply for getting money is no *karmayoga*, since the idea is simply to earn money. Cleaning of latrines for earning money is no *yajna* [sacrifice]. But the same act, if done by way of service, for the sake of sanitation and for the good of others, becomes *yajna*. One who does physical labor out of a spirit of service, in all humility and for self-realization, gets self-realization. Such a person would never feel reluctant to work. He should ever be tireless.

*　　*　　*

If we wish to develop in us the capacity to look on all as equals, we should also aim at getting only what the rest of the world gets. Thus, if the whole world gets milk, we may also have it. We may pray to God and say, "O God, if you wish me to have milk, give it first to the rest of the world." But who can pray thus? Only he who has so much sympathy for others and who labors for their good. Even if we cannot practice this principle, we must at least understand and appreciate it.

For the present, our only prayer to God should be that, since we are fallen so low, he should accept whatever little we are capable of doing. Even if we do not progress very far in this direction, he should give us strength to lessen our possessions. If we repent of our sins, they will at least not increase further. We should not keep anything with us thinking it as our own, but should strive to give up as many of our possessions as we can.

☆   ☆   ☆

Passionate desire is common both to man and woman. The mind of such a person always wanders about seeking an object of pleasure. But we must understand that we have obtained this birth not for enjoying or giving such pleasures, but for self-realization.

☆   ☆   ☆

There is no meaning in our observing sacred days and vows without understanding their significance. Such observance becomes useful both to us and to society if we understand its meaning and can explain it to others. Our women observe Nagapanchami, Janmashtami, and other holy days. But they should understand why they are observing them. It is possible that the meaning of Nagapanchami is to regard the serpent as the symbol of one's enemy and it was sought through this means to inculcate the principle that one should not kill even one's enemy. In this world, there is no other creature so poisonous to man as a serpent except another man. If we find any one as full of venom as a serpent, we should learn to love him, as though he were full of nectar. From doing this, we shall learn that every human being is worthy of worship, i.e. of service.

☆   ☆   ☆

Instead of training women to use a dagger, it is better to teach them to be fearless. God's protecting hands are always over us. If we really believe in the existence of God, whom shall we fear? Even if the most wicked of persons assaults you, take Ramanama [the name of God]. Most wicked persons would run away at this earnest cry to God. But if that does not happen, what does it matter? We should learn to die on such an occasion.

Bapu's Letters to Ashram Sisters (1960), pp. 94-114

Part III.
Ramanama:
Repetition of God's Name

77. How to Recite Ramanama

Gandhiji in today's discourse explained the conditions under which alone Ramanama could become an effective remedy. The first condition was that it should come from the heart. What did that mean? People did not mind going to the ends of the earth to find a cure for their physical ailments, which were much less important than the mental or spiritual. "Man's physical being is after all perishable. It cannot, by its very nature, last for ever. And yet men make a fetish of it while neglecting the immortal spirit within." A man who believed in Ramanama would not make a fetish of the body, but would regard it only as a means of serving God. And for making it into a fit instrument for that purpose, Ramanama was the sovereign means.

To install Ramanama in the heart required infinite patience. It might even take ages. But the effort was worthwhile. Even so, success depended solely on the grace of God.

Ramanama could not come from the heart unless one had cultivated the virtues of truth, honesty and purity within and without. Every day at the evening prayers, they repeated the shlokas describing the man with a steadfast intellect. Every one of them, said Gandhiji, could become a *sthataprajna* — man with steadfast intellect — if he kept his senses under discipline, and ate and drank and allowed himself enjoyment and recreation only to sustain life for service. If one had no control over one's thoughts; if one did not mind sleeping in a hole of a room with all doors and windows shut, and breathing foul air or drinking dirty water, his recitation of Ramanama was in vain.

That, however, did not mean that one should give up reciting Ramanama on the ground that one had not the requisite purity. For recitation of Ramanama was also a means for acquiring purity. "In the case of a man who repeats Ramanama from the heart, discipline and self control will come easy. Observance of the rules of health and hygiene will become his second nature. His life will run an even course. He will never want to hurt anyone. To suffer in order to relieve other's suffering will become a part of his being and fill him with an ineffable and perennial joy."

Let them, therefore, said Gandhiji, persevere and ceaselessly repeat Ramanama during all their waking hours. Ultimately, it would remain with them even during their sleep, and God's grace would then fill them with perfect health of body, mind and spirit.

Prayer Speech, New Delhi, May 25, 1946

78. A Good Seed Sown

From my sixth or seventh year up to my sixteenth I was at school, being taught all sorts of things except religion. I may say that I failed to get from the teachers what they could have given me without any effort on their part. And yet I kept on picking up things here and there from my surroundings. The term religion I am using in its broadest sense, meaning thereby self-realization or knowledge of self.

Being born in the Vaishnava faith, I had often to go to the *haveli* [temple]. But it never appealed to me. I did not like its glitter and pomp. Also I heard rumours of immorality being practised there, and lost all interest in it. Hence, I could gain nothing from the *haveli*.

But what I failed to get there I obtained from my nurse, an old servant of the family, whose affection for me I still recall.

There was in me a fear of ghosts and spirits. Rambha, for that was her name, suggested, as a remedy for this fear, the repetition of Ramanama. I had more faith in her than in her remedy, and so at a tender age I began repeating Ramanama to cure my fear of ghosts and spirits. This was, of course, short-lived; but the good seed sown in childhood was not sown in vain. I think it is due to the seed sown by that good woman Rambha that today Ramanama is an infallible remedy for me.

Autobiography (1969), pp. 22-23

79. Who is Rama?

You ask what is Rama. I may explain to you the meaning of that word, but then your repetition of that name would be nearly fruitless. But if you understand that Rama is he whom you intend to worship and then repeat his name, it will serve the purpose of the horn of plenty for you. You may repeat it like a parrot, but still it will be helpful because your repetition, unlike the parrot's, is backed by a purpose. Thus you do not need any symbol, and Tulsidas holds that the name of Rama is more powerful than Rama himself and suggests that there is no relation between the word Rama and its meaning. The meaning will be filled in later by the devotee in accordance with the nature of his devotion.

That is the beauty of this repetition. Otherwise, it would be impossible to prove that it will make a new man even of a simpleton. The devotee must fulfil only a single condition. The name should not be repeated for show or with a view to deceiving others, but with determination and faith. If a man perseveres with such repetition, I have not the shadow of a doubt that it will be for him a universal provider. Every one who has the requisite patience can realize this in his own case.

For days and sometimes for years, the mind wanders and becomes restless. The body craves for sleep when one is engaged in repeating the name. Indeed even still more painful symptoms intervene. Still if the seeker perseveres with the repetition, it is bound to bear fruit. Spinning is a gross material accomplishment and yet it can be acquired only after our patience is sorely tried. Things more difficult than spinning demand a greater effort on our part. Therefore he who is out to attain the supreme must undergo the necessary discipline for a long, long time and never be downhearted.

I think I have now answered all your questions. If you have faith, repeat the name at all times, when you sit or stand or lie down, eat or drink. There is no reason to despair if the whole of your lifetime is spent while you are at it. If you try it, you will have peace of mind in an increasing measure.

The Diary of Mahadev Desai, vol. I (1953), pp. 120-21

Q: You have often said that when you talk of Rama you refer to the ruler of the universe and not to Rama, the son of Dasharatha. But we find that your Ramadhun calls on Sita Rama and Raja Rama and it ends with "Victory to Rama, the Lord of Sita." Who is this Rama if not the son of the King Dasharatha?

A: I have answered such questions before, but there is something new in this one. It demands a reply. In *Ramadhun* "Raja Rama" and "Sita Rama" are undoubtedly repeated. Is not this Rama the same as the son of Dasharatha? Tulsidas has answered this question. But let me put down my own view. More potent than Rama is the name. Hindu Dharma is like a boundless ocean teeming with priceless gems. The deeper you dive the more treasures you find. In Hindu religion God is known by various names. Thousands of people look doubtless upon Rama and Krishna as historical figures and literally believe that God came down in person on earth in the form of Rama, the son of Dasharatha, and by worshipping him one can attain salvation. The same thing holds good about Krishna.

History, imagination and truth have got so inextricably

mixed up. It is next to impossible to disentangle them. I have accepted all the names and forms attributed to God as symbols connoting one formless omnipresent Rama. To me, therefore, Rama, described as the Lord of Sita, son of Dasharatha, is the all powerful essence whose name, inscribed in the heart, removes all suffering — mental, moral and physical.

Harijan, June 2, 1946

80. Power of Ramanama

Ramanama ought to be repeated from the depth of one's heart; it would not then matter if the words are not pronounced correctly. The broken words which proceed from the heart are acceptable in God's court. Even though the heart cries out "Mara, mara," [Rama pronounced in reverse; "Dying, dying"] this appeal of the heart will be recorded in one's credit column. On the contrary, though the tongue may pronounce the name of Rama correctly, if the lord of that heart is Ravana, the correct repetition of Rama's name will be recorded in one's debit column.

Tulsidas did not sing the glory of Ramanama for the benefit of the hypocrite "who has Rama's name on his. lips and a knife under his arm." His wise calculations will go wrong, while the seeming errors of the man who has installed Rama in his heart will succeed. Rama alone can repair one's fortunes and so the poet Surdas, Lover of God, sings:

Who will repair my fortunes?
O who else but Rama?
Everyone is a friend of his on whom good fortune smiles,
None of his whom fortune has forsaken.

The reader, therefore, should understand clearly that Ramanama is a matter of the heart. Where speech and the mind are not in harmony with each other, mere speech is falsehood, no more than pretence or play of words. Such chanting may well deceive the world, but can Rama who dwells in man's heart be deceived?

Hanuman broke open the beads in the necklace which Sita gave him as a gift, wanting to see whether they were inscribed with Rama's name. Some courtiers who thought themselves wise asked him why he showed disrespect to Sita's necklace. Hanuman's reply was that if the beads were not inscribed with Rama's name inside, then every necklace given to him by Sita was a burden to him. The wise courtiers thereupon smilingly asked him if Rama's name was inscribed in his heart. Hanuman drew out his knife and, cutting open his chest, said, "Now look inside. Tell me if you see anything else there except Rama's name." The courtiers felt ashamed. Flowers rained on Hanuman from the sky, and from that day Hanuman's name is always invoked when Rama's story is recited. This may be only a legend or a dramatist's invention. Its moral is valid for all time: only that which is in one's heart is true.

Collected Works — XXVII (1968), pp. 111-12

For one who has never experienced peace and is in quest of it, Ramanama will certainly prove a [philosopher's stone]. God has been given a thousand names, which only means that he can be called by any name and that his qualities are infinite. That is why God is also beyond nomenclature and free from attributes. But for us mortals the support of his name is absolutely essential to fall back upon and in this age even the ignorant and the illiterate can have recourse to an Ekakshara mantra ["Om"] in the form of Ramanama. In fact, uttering Ramanama covers the Ekakshara and there is no difference between "Om" and "Rama." But the value of reciting his name cannot be established by reasoning, it can only be experienced if one does it with faith.

Collected Works — XXXIV (1969), pp. 162-63

If you repeat the name of Rama on getting up in the morning and before going to bed in the evening the day will go well for you and the night pass without bad dreams.
Collected Works — XXVI (1967),

81. A Well-Tried Formula

It is easy enough to take a vow under a stimulating influence. But it is difficult to keep to it, especially in the midst of temptation. God is our only help in such circumstances. I therefore suggested to the meeting [of elders in the village of Vedchhi] Ramanama. Rama, Allah and God are to me convertible terms. I had discovered that simple people deluded themselves in the belief that I appeared to them in their distress. I wanted to remove the superstition. I knew that I appeared to nobody. It was pure hallucination for them to rely on a frail rnortal. I therefore presented them with a simple and well-tried formula that has never failed, namely to invoke the assistance of God every morning before sunrise, and every evening before bed time, for the fulfilment of the vows. Millions of Hindus know him under the name of Rama. As a child, I was taught to call upon Rama when I was seized with fear. I know many of my companions to whom Ramanama has been of the greatest solace in the hour of their need. I presented it to the Dharalas [a military tribe in Gujarat] and to the untouchables. I present it also to the reader whose vision is not blurred and whose faith is not damped by overmuch learning. Learning takes us through many stages in life but it fails us utterly in the hour of danger and temptation. Then faith alone saves. Ramanama is not for those who tempt God in every way possible and ever expect it to save. It is for those who walk in the fear of God, who want to restrain themselves and cannot in spite of themselves.
Young India, January 22, 1925

82. Ridiculing Ramanama

Q: You know, we are so ignorant and dull that we actually begin to worship the images of our great men instead of living up to their teachings. The recently opened Gandhi temple is a living testimony of that. The Ramanama bank in Banaras and wearing clothes printed with Ramanama is, in my opinion, a caricature and even insult of Ramanama. Don't you think that under these circumstances your telling the people to take to Ramanama as a sovereign remedy for all ailments is likely to encourage ignorance and hypocrisy? Ramanama repeated from the heart can be a sovereign remedy, but in my opinion religious education of the right type alone can lead to that state.

A: You are right. There is so much superstition and hypocrisy around that one is afraid even to do the right thing. But if one gives way to fear, even truth will have to be suppressed. The golden rule is to act fearlessly upon what one believes to be right. Hypocrisy and untruth will go on in the world. Our doing the right thing will result in their decrease, never in their increase. The danger is that when we are surrounded by falsehood on all sides we might be caught in it and begin to deceive ourselves. We should be careful not to make a mistake out of our laziness and ignorance. Constant vigilance under all circumstances is essential. A votary of truth cannot act otherwise. Even an all-power remedy like Ramanama can become useless for lack of wakefulness and care, and become one more addition to the numerous current superstitions.

Harijan, June 2, 1946

83. Ramanama Must Not Cease

Q: While in conversation or doing brain work or when one is suddenly worried, can one recite Ramanama in one's heart? Do people do so at such times, and if so, how?

A: Experience shows that man can do so at any time, even in sleep, provided Ramanama is enshrined in his heart. If the taking of the name has become a habit, its recitation through the heart becomes as natural as the heart beat. Otherwise, Ramanama is a mere mechanical performance or at best has touched the heart only on the surface. When Ramanama has established its dominion over the heart, the question of vocal recitation does not arise. Because then it transcends speech. But it may well be held that persons who have attained this state are few and far between.

There is no doubt whatsoever that Ramanama contains all the power that is attributed to it. No one can, by mere wishing, enshrine Ramanama in his heart. Untiring effort is required as also patience. What an amount of labor and patience have been lavished by men to acquire the non-existent philosopher's stone? Surely, God's name is of infinitely richer value and always existent.

Q: Is it harmful if, owing to stress or exigencies of work, one is unable to carry out daily devotions in the prescribed manner? Which of the two should be given preference? Service or the rosary?

A: Whatever the exigencies of service or adverse circumstances may be, Ramanama must not cease. The outward form will vary according to the occasion. The absence of the rosary does not interrupt Ramanama which has found an abiding place in the heart.

Harijan, February 17, 1946

84. Ramanama and National Service

Q: Can a man or woman attain self-realization by mere recitation of Ramanama and without taking part in national service? I ask this question because some of my sisters say that they do not need to do anything beyond attending to family requirements, and occasionally showing kindness to the poor.

A: This question has puzzled not only women, but many men, and has taxed me to the utmost. I know that there is a school of philosophy which teaches complete inaction and futility of all effort. I have not been able to appreciate that teaching, unless in order to secure verbal agreement I were to put my own interpretation on it. In my humble opinion, effort is necessary for one's own growth. It has to be irrespective of results. Ramanama or some equivalent is necessary, not for the sake of repetition, but for the sake of purification, as an aid to effort, for direct guidance from above. It is, therefore, never a substitute for effort. It is meant for intensifying and guiding it in proper channels.

If all effort is vain, why family cares or an occasional help to the poor? In this very effort is contained the germ of national service. And national service, to me, means service of humanity, even as disinterested service of the family means the same thing. Disinterested service of the family, necessarily, leads one to national service. Ramanama gives one detachment and ballast, and never throws one off one's balance at critical moments. Self-realization I hold to be impossible without service of, and identification with, the poorest.

Young India, October 21, 1926

85. Ramanama and Nature Cure

You will be pleased to know that I became a confirmed convert to Nature Cure when I read Kuhne's *New Science of Healing* and Just's *Return to Nature* over forty years ago. I must confess that I have not been able fully to follow the meaning of *Return to Nature* not because of want of will but because of my ignorance. I am now trying to evolve a system of Nature Cure suited to the millions of India's poor. I try to confine myself to the propagation of such cure as is derivable from the use of earth, water, light, air and the great void. This naturally leads man to know that the sovereign cure of all ills is the recitation from the heart of the name of God whom some millions here know by the name of Rama and the other millions by the name of Allah. Such recitation from the heart carries with it the obligation to recognize and follow the laws which nature has ordained for man. This train of reasoning leads one to the conclusion that prevention is better than cure. Therefore, one is irresistibly driven to inculcating the laws of hygiene, i.e., of cleanliness of the mind, of the body and of its surroundings.

Harijan, June 15, 1947

My conception of Nature Cure, like everything else, has undergone a progressive evolution. And for years I have believed that if a person is filled with the presence of God and has thus attained the state of dispassion, he can surmount handicaps against long life. I have come to the conclusion, based on observation and scriptural reading, that when a man comes to that complete living faith in the unseen power and has become free from passion, the body undergoes internal transformation. This does not come about by mere wish. It needs constant vigilance and practice. In spite of both, unless God's grace descends upon one, human effort comes to naught.

Press Report, June 12, 1945

Nature Cure treatment means that treatment which befits man. By "man" is meant not merely man as an animal, but as a creature possessing, in addition to his body, both mind and soul. For such a being Ramanama is the truest Nature Cure treatment. It is an unfailing remedy. The expression "Ramabana" or infallible cure is derived from it. Nature, too, indicates that for man it is the worthy remedy. No matter what the ailment from which a man may be suffering, recitation of Ramanama from the heart is the sure cure. God has many names. Each person can choose the name that appeals most to him. Ishwara, Allah, Khuda, God mean the same. But the recitation must not be parrot-like, it must be born of faith. . . .

Man should seek out and be content to confine the means of cure to the five elements of which the body is composed, i.e., earth, water, akash [space], sun and air. Of course, Ramanama must be the invariable accompaniment. If in spite of this, death supervenes, we may not mind. On the contrary, it should be welcomed. Science has not so far discovered any recipe for making the body immortal. Immortality is an attribute of the soul. That is certainly imperishable, but it is man's duty to try to express its purity.

Harijan, March 3, 1946

Shri Ganeshshastri Joshi, vaidya [physician], tells me after reading the above article, that in Ayurveda, too, there is ample testimony to the efficacy of Ramanama as a cure for all disease. Nature Cure occupies the place of honor and in it Ramanama is the most important. When Charaka, Vagbhata and other giants of medicine in ancient India wrote, the popular name for God was not Rama but Vishnu. I myself have been a devotee of Tulsidas from my childhood and have, therefore, always worshipped God as Rama. But I know that if, beginning with Omkar, one goes through the entire gamut of God's names current in all climes, all countries and all languages, the result is the same. He and his law are one. To observe his law is, therefore, the best form of worship. A man who becomes one with the law does not stand in need of vocal recitation of the name. In other words, an individual with whom contemplation on God has become as natural as breathing is so filled with God's spirit that knowledge or observance of the law becomes second nature, as it were, with him. Such an one needs no other treatment.

The question, then, arises as to why, in spite of having the prince of remedies at hand, we know so little about it; and why even those who know, do not remember him or remember him only by lip-service, not from the heart. . . .

This sovereign remedy is not administered by doctors, vaidyas, hakims or any other medical practitioners. These have no faith in it. If they were to admit that the spring of the holy Ganga could be found in every home, their very occupation or means of livelihood would go. Therefore, they must perforce rely on their powders and potions as infallible remedies. Not only do these provide bread for the doctor, but the patient, too, seems to feel immediate relief. If a medical practitioner can get a few persons to say, "So and so gave me a powder and I was cured," his business is established.

Nor, it must be borne in mind, would it really be of any use for doctors to prescribe God's name to patients unless they themselves were conscious of its miraculous powers. Ramanama is no copy-book maxim. It is something that has to be realized through experience. One who has had personal experience alone can prescribe it, not any other.

Harijan, March 24, 1946

I have no doubt whatsoever that the spread of Ramanama and pure living are the best and cheapest preventives of disease. The tragedy is that doctors, hakims and vaidyas do not make use of Ramanama as the sovereign of cures. There is no place given to it in current Ayurvedic literature, except it be in the shape of a charm which will drive people further into the well of superstition. Ramanama has, in fact, no connection with superstition. It is nature's supreme law. Whoever observes it is free from disease and *vice versa*. The same law which keeps one free from disease, applies also to its cure.

An apt question is as to why a man who recites Ramanama regularly and leads a pure life should ever fall ill. Man is by nature imperfcct. A thoughtful man strives after perfection, but never attains it. He stumbles on the way, however, unwittingly.

The whole of God's law is embodied in a pure life. The first thing is to realize one's limitations. It should be obvious that the moment one transgresses those limits, one falls ill. Thus, a balanced diet eaten in accordance with needs gives one freedom from disease. How is one to know what is the proper diet for one? Many such enigmas can be imagined. The purport of it all is that everyone should be his own doctor and find out his limitations. The man who does so will surely live up to 125.

Doctor friends claim that they do nothing more than investigate the laws and act accordingly and that, therefore, they are the best Nature Cure men. Everything can be explained away in this manner. All I want to say is that anything more than Ramanama is really contrary to true Nature Cure. The more one recedes from this central principle, the farther away one goes from Nature Cure.

Following this line of thought, I limit Nature Cure to the use of the five elements. But a vaidya who goes beyond this and uses such herbs as grow or can be grown in his neighbourhood, purely for service of the sick and not for money, may claim to be a Nature Cure man. But where are such vaidyas to be found? Today most of them are engaged in making money. They do no research work and it is because of their greed and mental laziness that the science of Ayurveda is at a low ebb.

Harijan, May 19, 1946

My mother gave me medicines so far as I remember. But she did believe in spells and charms. Learned friends have faith in them. I have not. There is no connection between Ramanama of my conception and charms. I have said that to take Ramanama from the heart means deriving help from an incomparable power. The atom bomb is as nothing compared with it. This power is capable of removing all pain.

It must, however, be admitted that it is easy to say that Ramanama must come from the heart, but to attain the reality is very difficult. Nevertheless, it is the biggest thing man can possess.
Harijan, October 13, 1946

86. The Sovereign Remedy

In his after-prayer speech Gandhiji referred to several letters and messages from friends expressing concern over his persistent cough. His speech was broadcast, and so was the cough which was often troublesome in the evening and in the open. For the last four days, however, the cough had been on the whole less troublesome and he hoped it would soon disappear completely. The reason for the persistence of the cough had been that he had refused all medical treatment. Dr. Sushila had said that if at the outset he had taken penicillin he would have been all right in three days. Otherwise, it would take him three weeks to get over it. He did not doubt the efficacy of penicillin but he believed too that Ramanama was the sovereign remedy for all ills and, therefore, superseded all other remedies. In the midst of the flames that surrounded him on all sides, there was all the greater need for a burning faith in God. God alone could enable people to put down the fire. If He had to take work from Gandhiji, He would keep him alive. Otherwise He would carry him away.

They had just heard the *bhajan* in which the poet had exhorted man to stick to Ramanama. He alone was the refuge of man. Therefore, in the present crisis he wished to throw himself entirely on God and not accept medical aid for a physical ailment.
Ramanama (1964), pp. 47-57

87. Misuse of Ramanama

In his after-prayer discourse, Gandhiji again dwelt on the subject of Nature Cure or the cure of ailments spiritual, mental and physical, by the application principally of Ramanama. A correspondent had written to him, pointing out how some people superstitiously wrote Ramanama on their clothes so as to wear it next to the heart! Others wrote Ramanama millions of times minutely on a piece of paper which they afterwards cut up into small bits and swallowed so that they could claim that Ramanama had entered into them! There were people who thought that he was self-deluded and was trying to delude others by adding one more to the thousands of superstitions which filled this superstition-ridden land. He had no answer to such criticism. He only said to himself, what did it matter if truth was abused and fraud practised in its name by others? So long as he was sure of his truth, he could not help proclaiming it for fear of its being misunderstood or abused. "Nobody in this world possesses absolute truth. This is God's attribute alone. Relative truth is all we know. Therefore, we can only follow the truth as we see it. Such pursuit of truth cannot lead anyone astray."

Prayer Spech, New Delhi, May 24, 1946

Part IV.
Last Breath

88. God, the Only Protector

Ever since I took the pledge of service I have dedicated my head to humanity. It is the easiest thing in the world to chop off my head, it does not take the slightest preparation or organization. And outside protection I have never sought. In fact it is futile to think of protecting me for I know that God Almighty is the only protector.

> *Homage to the Departed* (1958) p. 198

A warrior loves to die, not on a sick-bed but on the battle-field. . . . Death is at any time blessed, but it is twice blessed for a warrior who dies for his cause, i.e. truth.

> *Young India*, December 30, 1926

Buddha would have died resisting the priesthood if the majesty of his love had not proved to be equal to the task of bending the priesthood. Christ died on the cross with a crown of thorns on his head, defying the might of a whole empire. And if I raise the resistance of a nonviolent character, I simply and humbly follow in the footsteps of the great teachers.

> *Young India*, May 12, 1920

I am not aching for martyrdom, but if it comes my way in the prosecution of what I consider to be the supreme duty in the defence of the faith that I hold. . . . I shall have earned it.

> *Harijan*, June 29, 1934

I hope there will be nonviolent non-cooperators enough in India of whom it will be written, "They suffered bullets without anger and with prayer on their lips even for the ignorant murderer."
A Gandhi Anthology, Book I (1958), p. 9

If someone killed me and I died with prayer for the assassin on my lips, and God's remembrance and consciousness of his living presence in the sanctuary of my heart, then alone would I be said to have had the nonviolence of the brave.
Mahatma Gandhi, The Last Phase, vol. II (1958), p. 327

I believe in the message of truth delivered by all the religious teachers of the world. And it is my constant prayer that I may never have a feeling of anger against my traducers, that even if I fall victim to an assassin's bullet, I may deliver up my soul with the remembrance of God upon my lips. I shall be content to be written down an impostor if my lips utter a word of anger or abuse against my assailant at the last moment.
Mahatma Gandhi, The Last Phase, vol. II (1958), p. 101

I do not want to die . . . of a creeping paralysis of my faculties — a defeated man. An assassin's bullet may put an end to my life. I would welcome it. But I would love, above all, to fade out doing my duty with my last breath.
Mahatma Gandhi, The Last Phase, vol. I (1956), p. 562

(To Manubehn Gandhi on the night of January 29, 1948, less than twenty hours before his assasination)
You know my faith in Ramanama. If I die due to a lingering illness, nay even by as much as a boil or a pimple, it will be your duty to proclaim to the world, even at the risk of making people angry at you, that I was not the man of God that I claimed to be. If you do that my spirit will have peace. Note down this also: That if someone were to end my life by putting a bullet through

me, as someone tried to do with a bomb the other day, and I met this bullet without a groan, and breathed my last taking God's name, then alone would I have made good my claim.

The End of An Epoch (1962), pp. 28-29

[To Manubehn Gandhi just twelve hours before his assassination] If someone fires bullets at me and I die without a groan and with God's name on my lips then you should tell the world that he was a real Mahatma.

The End of An Epoch (1962), p. 32

Even if I am killed, I will not give up repeating the names of Rama and Rahim which mean to me the same God. With these names on my lips I will die cheerfully.

Homage to The Departed (1958), p. 196

89. Rama! Rama!

(By Pyarelal)
As Gandhiji passed through the cordoned lane through the prayer congregation, he took his hands off the shoulders of the two girls to answer the *namaskars* of the prayer congregation. All of a sudden some one from the crowd roughly elbowed his way into the cordon from the right. Little Manu, thinking that he was coming forward to touch his feet, remonstrated saying something about it being already late for the prayer and tried to stop the intruder by holding his hand. He violently jerked her off, causing the *Ashram Bhajanavali* and Bapu's spittoon and mala, which she was carrying in her hands, to fall down. As she stooped down to pick up the scattered things, he planted himself in front of Bapu at less than point blank range — so close, indeed, that one of the ejected shells was afterwards found caught among the folds of Bapu's clothes. Three shots rang out in quick succession from

the seven-chambered automatic pistol, the first shot entering the abdomen on the right side two and a half inches above the umbilicus and three and a half inches to the right of the mid line, the second penetrating the seventh intercostal space one inch to the right of the mid line and the third on the right side of the chest one inch above the nipple and four inches from the mid line. The first and the second shots passed right through and came out at the back. The third remained embedded in the lung. At the first shot the foot that was in motion, when he was hit, came down. He still stood on his legs when the second shot rang out and then collapsed. The last words he uttered were "Rama, Rama."

Harijan, February 15, 1948

Appendices

Appendix A.
Selected Ashram Prayers

Morning Prayers

Early in the morning I call to mind
that being which is felt in the heart
which is *sat, chit* and *sukham,*
the eternal, knowledge and bliss,
which is the state reached by perfect men,
and which is the super-state.
I am that immaculate Brahma
which ever notes the states of dream,
wakefulness and deep sleep,
not this body, the compound made of
the elements — earth, water, space, light and air.

In the early morning I worship him
who is beyond the reach
of thought and speech,
and yet by whose grace all speech is possible.
I worship him whom the Vedas describe
as *neti, neti* — not this, not this.
Him they, the sages, have called
God of gods, the unborn,
the unfallen, the source of all.

In the early morning I bow to him
who is beyond darkness,
who is like the sun,
who is perfect, ancient,

called Purushottama, the best among men,
and in whom, through the veil of darkness,
we fancy the whole universe as appearing,
even as, in darkness,
we imagine a rope to be a snake.

O! goddess Earth
with the ocean for thy garment,
mountains for thy breasts,
thou consort of Vishnu, the Preserver,
I bow to thee.
Forgive the touch of my feet.

May the goddess of learning, Sarasvati,
the destroyer completely of black ignorance,
protect me—
she who is white as the mogra flower
or the moon and a garland of snow,
who has worn white robes,
whose hands are adorned
with the beautiful bamboo of her veena,
who is seated on a white lotus,
and who is always adored
by Brahma, Vishnu, Siva and the other gods.

Guru is Brahma,
he is Vishnu,
he is Mahadev,
he is the great Brahman itself.
I bow to that guru.
I bow to Vishnu, who is peace incarnate,
who lies on a snaky bed,
from whose navel grows the lotus,
who is the supreme lord of the gods,

who sustains the universe,
who is like unto the sky,
who has the color of clouds,
whose body is blissful,
who is the lord of Lakshmi [goddess of good fortune],
who has lotus-like eyes,
who is knowable by the *yogis* through meditation,
who dispels the fear of the wheel of birth and death,
and who is the sole Ruler of all the worlds.

Forgive, O merciful and blessed Mahadev,
all those sins of mine of commission or omission,
mental or actual, and whether done through
the hands or the feet, the speech, the ears or the eyes.
Let thy will be done.

I desire neither earthly kingdom nor paradise,
no, not even release from birth and death.
I desire only the release of afflicted life from misery.

Blessed be the people.
May the rulers protect
their kingdoms by just means.
May it be always well
with the cow and the brahmin.
May all the peoples be happy.

I bow to thee the *sat*, the cause of the universe.
I bow to thee the *chit*, the refuge of the world.
I bow to thee the one without a second, the giver
    of salvation.
I bow to thee the Brahman, the all-pervading, the eternal.

—————————

Thou art the only refuge.
Thou art the only one to be desired.
Thou art the sole protector of the universe.
Thou art self-revealed.
Thou art the sole creator, preserver and destroyer of the uni-
    verse.
Thou alone art supreme, immovable, unchangeable.

Of all the fears, thou art the chief.
Of all that is terrible thou art the most terrible.
Thou art the motion of all life.
Thou art the holy of holies.
Thou art the sole regulator of the mightiest places.
Thou art the greatest among the great.
Thou art the chief among all protections.

We think of thee, we worship thee,
we bow to thee as the witness of this universe.
We seek refuge in thee, the *sat*;
our only support, yet thyself needing none;
the ruler, the bark in the midst of this ocean
of endless birth and death.

Kumar Mandir Prayer

Om!
May God protect us,
may he support us,
may we make joint progress,
may our studies be fruitful,
may we never harbor ill will
against one another.
Om shanti, shanti, shanti.

Om!
From untruth lead me unto truth,
from darkness lead me unto light,
from death lead me unto life everlasting.

I bow to thee, O God,
who, being almighty and having entered my heart,
gives by his power life to the silent tongue, the hands,
feet, ears, skin and other members of the body.

Prayer of Tukaram

Lord, preserve me from looking on things which arouse thoughts.
    It were better for me to be blind.
Lord, preserve me from soiling my lips with impure words.
    It were better for me to be dumb.
Lord, preserve me from hearing any word of slander and insult.
    It were better for me to be deaf.
Lord, preserve me from looking with desire on any of those who
    should be my sisters.
It were better for me to be dead.

Women's Prayers

O Govind, dweller of Dwarika,
Krishna, thou beloved of the Gopis,
O Keshav, dost thou not know
that the Kauravas have surrounded me?
O Lord, thou lord of Lakshmi,
protector of Vraja, deliverer from affliction,
O Janardana, save me from the ocean
of misery in the shape of the Kauravas.
O Krishna, thou great Yogi,
soul and protector of the universe,
O Govind, deliver me lying hopeless
in the midst of the Kauravas and seeking thy support.

Act righteously, never unrighteously;
speak truth, never untruth;
look far ahead, never shortsightedly;
look above, never below.

Ahimsa, truth, non-stealing, purity and self-control,
these, said Manu, are the common duty of all the four
    divisions.

Ahimsa, truth, non-stealing, freedom from passion, anger and
    greed,
wishing the well-being and good of all that lives,
these are the duty common to all the divisions.

Understand that to be religion
which the wise, the good and those that are free
from likes and dislikes follow
and which is felt in the heart.

Listen to the essence of religion
and assimilate it through the heart:
one should never do to others
which one would not wish done to oneself.
That which has been said in countless books
I shall say in half a verse:
service of others is virtue, injury to others is sin.

The sun, the moon, the wind, the fire,
the sky, the earth, the waters, the heart,
the god of judgment, the day, the night,
the evening, the morning and dharma itself
are witnesses to man's actions.
He can conceal nothing.

Prayer of Surdas

Who can be so crooked, bad or dissolute as I?
I am so faithless that I have forgotten
the very God who gave me this body.
Even like the village dog
I have been fattening myself and running after pleasures.
I have given up the company of God's people,
and day and night slave for those who revile him.
Who can be a greater sinner than I?
I am the chief among them.
Surdas says, O God, listen,
where is the resting place for a sinner like me?

Appendix B.
Favorite Hymns

The True Vashnava

He is a real Vaishnava,
who feels the suffering of others as his own suffering.
He is ever ready to serve,
and is never guilty of overweening pride.
He bows before everyone, despises none,
preserves purity in thought, word and deed.
Blessed is the mother of such a son;
in every woman he reveres his mother.
He preserves equanimity and never stains his mouth
with falsehood, nor touches the riches of another.
The bonds of desire cannot hold him.
Ever in harmony with Ramanama,
his body in itself possesses all the places of pilgrimage.
He knows neither desire nor disappointment,
neither passion nor wrath.
    — *Narasimha Mehta*

Path of Love

The way of the Lord is open only to heroes, to cowards it is fast
    shut.
Give up thy life and all that thou hast, so thou mayst assume the
    name of the Lord.
Only he who leaves his son, his wife, his riches, and his life, shall
    drink from the vessel of God.

For in truth, he that would fish for pearls must dive into the
deepest depths of the sea and take his life in his hands.
Death affrights him not; he forgets all the misery of body and
soul.
He who stands hesitating on the bank and fears to dive, gains
nought.
But the path of love is trial by fire. The coward shrinks back
from it.
He who dares the leap into the fire, attains to everlasting bliss.
— *Pritama*

Lead Kindly Light

Lead, kindly light, amid the encircling gloom,
Lead thou me on.
The night is dark, and I am far from home;
Lead thou me on.
Keep thou my feet; I do not ask to see
The distant scene; one step enough for me.
I was not ever thus, nor pray'd that thou
Shouldst lead me on.
I loved to choose, and see my path; but now
Lead thou me on.
I loved the garish day, and, spite of fears,
Pride ruled my will: remember not past years.
So long Thy power hath blest me. Sure it still
Will lead me on.
O'er moor and fen, o'er crag and torrent,
The night is gone;
And with the morn those Angel faces smile,
Which I have loved long since, and lost awhile.
— *Cardinal John Henry Newman*

The Wondrous Cross

When I survey the wondrous cross
    On which the prince of glory died,
My richest gain I count but loss,
    And pour contempt on all my pride.
Forbid it, Lord, that I should boast
    Save in the cross of Christ, my God;
All the vain things that charm me most,
    I sacrifice them to His Blood.
See from his head, his hands, his feet,
    Sorrow and love flow mingling down;
Did e'er such love and sorrow meet,
    Or thorns compose so rich a crown?
Were the whole realm of nature mine,
    That were an offering far too small;
Love so amazing, so divine,
    Demands my soul, my life, my all.
To Christ, who won for sinners grace
    By bitter grief and anguish sore,
Be praise from all the ransom'd race,
    For ever and evermore.
    — *Isaac Watts*

Rock of Ages

Rock of ages, cleft for me,
Let me hide myself in thee;
Let the water and the blood,
From thy riven side which flowed,
Be of sin the double cure,
Cleanse me from its guilt and power.

Not the labors of my hands
Can fulfill thy law's demands;
Could my zeal no respite know,
Could my tears forever flow,
All for sin could not atone;
Thou must save, and thou alone.

Nothing in my hand I bring,
Simply to thy cross I cling;
Naked, come to thee for dress;
Helpless, look to thee for grace;
Foul, I to the fountain fly;
Wash me, savior, or I die.

While I draw this fleeting breath,
When my eyelids close in death,
When I soar through tracts unknown,
See thee on thy judgment throne;
Rock of ages, cleft for me,
Let me hide myself in thee.
　　　— A. M. Toplady

Sermon on the Mount

Blessed are the poor in spirit: for theirs is the Kingdom of Heaven.
Blessed are they that mourn: for they shall be comforted.
Blessed are the meek: for they shall inherit the earth.
Blessed are they which do hunger and thirst after righteousness:
　　　for they shall be filled.
Blessed are the merciful: for they shall obtain mercy.
Blessed are the pure in heart: for they shall see God.

Blessed are the peacemakers: for they shall be called the children
of God.
Blessed are they which are persecuted for righteousness' sale, for
theirs is the Kingdom of Heaven.
— *Gospel of Matthew*

In All Things Thee to See

Teach me, my God and king,
In all things thee to see,
And what I do in anything,
To do it as for thee.
All may of thee partake,
Nothing can be so mean
Which with this tincture, "for thy sake,"
Will not grow bright and clean.
A servant with this clause
Makes drudgery divine;
Who sweeps a room as for thy laws
Makes that and th' action fine.
This is the famous stone
That turneth all to gold;
For that which God doth touch and own
Cannot for less be told.
— *George Herbert*

In Our Father's House at Last

I say to thee, do thou repeat
    To the first man thou mayest meet
In lane, highway or open street —
    That he and we and all men move
Under a canopy of love
    As broad as the blue sky above;
That doubt and trouble, fear and pain,
    And anguish all are shadows vain;
That death itself shall not remain;
    That weary deserts we may tread,
A dreary labyrinth may thread,
    Through dark ways underground be led,
Yet, if we all one Guide obey,
    The dreariest path, the darkest way
Shall issue out in heavenly day.
    And we on diverse shores now cast,
Shall meet, our perilous voyage past,
    All in our Father's house at last.
    — *Trench*

Sources

A Gandhi Anthology I (1958), Compiled by V. G. Desai.

An Autobiography or The Story of My Experments with Truth (1969), Translated from Gujarati by Mahadev Desai.

Ashram Observances in Action (1959).

Bapu, My Mother (1955), by Manubehn Gandhi.

Bapu's Letters to Ashram Sisters (1960), edited by Kakasaheb Kalelkar.

Bapu's Letters to Mira (1959).

Food for the Soul (1957), edited by Anand T. Hingorani.

Harijan (1933-1956), English language newspaper published by Gandhi.

Hind Swaraj or Indian Home Rule (1962).

Homage to the Departed (1958), Compiled and Edited by S. B. Kher.

Mahadevbhaini Diary, vol. II (Gujarati Edition, 1949), by Mahadev Desai; edited by Narahari Parikh.

Mahatma Gandhi, The Last Phase — vol.I, book 1 (1965),Vol.I I (1958), by Pyarelal.

My Dear Child: Letters to Esther Faering (1959).

My Memorable Moments with Bapu (1960), by Manubehn Gandhi.

Ramanama (1964).

Speeches and Writings of Mahatma Gandlti (G. A. Natesan & Co., 4th Edition).

Stray Glimpses of Bapu (1960), by Kakasaheb Kalelkar.

The Collected Works of Mahatma Gandhi (The Publication Division, Ministry of Information snd Broadcasting, Government of India).

The Diary of Mahadev Desai, vol. I (1953), by Mahadev Desai, Translated from Gujarati and edited by Valji Govindji Desai.

The End of an Epoch (1962), by Manubehn Gandhi, Translated from Gujarati by Gopalkrishna Gandhi.

The Gospel of Selfless Action or The Gita According to Gandhi (1969) by Mahadev Desai.

This Was Bapu (1959), Compiled by R. K. Prabhu.

Young India (1919-1931), English language newspaper published by Gandhi.

Contributors

M. K. GANDHI is regarded by many as a Hindu saint and the father of Indian independence. Born at Porbandar on October 2, 1869, he left India as a young man to study law in London. His legal career took him to South Africa in 1893, where he first became involved in political struggles, working to secure rights for Indian expatriates. He remained in South Africa for more than two decades, and it was during these years that his remarkable form of political reform through non-violence, which he called Satyagraha, was born.

Upon his return to India, Gandhi assumed a leadership role in the fight for Indian independence from Great Britain. He also worked tirelessly for religious toleration in India, which was divided by Hindu-Moslem antagonism, and for the destruction of the caste system, which codified class conflicts in ancient religious terms. Gandhi's role emerged not only as that of a political revolutionary, but also as a religious leader. As he insisted, he was a man of God first.

Indian independence from Britain was finally achieved on August 15, 1947. Five months later, on January 25, 1948, Gandhi was assassinated by a conservative Hindu.

MICHAEL N. NAGLER is Professor Emeritus of Classics and Comparative Literature at the University of California, Berkeley. He is the founder of the University's Peace and Conflict Studies Program, and currently teaches courses in nonviolence and meditation. Dr. Nagler is the author of *Is There No Other Way?: The Search for a Nonviolent Furture*, and, with Eknath Easwaran, an English edition of *The Upanishads*, as well as numerous articles on classics, myth, peace and mysticism. His book *Is There No Other Way: The Search for a Nonviolent Future*, will be published by Berkeley Hills Books in Fall 2000.

ARUN GANDHI is the fifth grandson of Mahatma Gandhi. Raised in South Africa at the Phoenix Ashram, a religious community established by his grandfather in 1904, he moved to India as a teenager in 1945, and lived with the Mahatma during the last years of his life. Dr. Gandhi is a former journalist, and with his wife, Sunanda, started India's Center for Social Unity, an organization dedicated to alleviating poverty and caste discrimination. The author of eight books, Dr. Gandhi has been a resident of the United States since 1987. He and his wife are founders of the M. K. Gandhi Institute for Nonviolence at Christian Brothers University in Memphis, Tennessee.

For other titles in the Berkeley Hills Books series of works by Mahatma Gandhi, please contact your bookseller, call us toll-free at (888) 848-7303, or see www.berkeleyhills.com.

The Bhagavad Gita According to Gandhi (Summer 2000)
Includes Mahadev Desai's English translation of Gandhi's Gujarati rendering of the Gita, with extensive notes and commentary by the Mahatma. ISBN: 1-893163-11-3

Book of Prayers
Selections from Gandhi's *Ashram Bhajanavali*, the prayer book of Satyagraha Ashram. Translated into English by Gandhi for his western followers. ISBN: 1-893163-02-4

Vows and Observances
Gandhi's writings on the "Eleven Observances," the rules for daily living of Satyagraha Ashram. ISBN: 1-893163-01-6

The Way to God
Selections from Gandhi's writings on the nature of God and spiritual practice. ISBN: 1-893163-00-8